Nurturing the Whole Student

Other Titles of Interest by Rowman & Littlefield Education

Nurturing the Whole Student

Five Dimensions of Teaching and Learning

Clifford Mayes and Ellen Williams

ROWMAN & LITTLEFIELD EDUCATION
A division of
ROWMAN & LITTLEFIELD PUBLISHERS, INC.
Lanham • New York • Toronto • Plymouth, UK

Published by Rowman & Littlefield Education
A division of Rowman & Littlefield Publishers, Inc.
A wholly owned subsidary of The Rowman & Littlefield Publishing Group, Inc.
4501 Forbes Boulevard, Suite 200, Lanham, Maryland 20706
www.rowman.com

10 Thornbury Road, Plymouth PL6 7PP, United Kingdom

British Library Cataloguing in Publication Information Available

Library of Congress Cataloging-in-Publication Data

Mayes, Clifford.
Nurturing the whole student : five dimensions of teaching and learning / Clifford Mayes and Ellen Williams.
p. cm.
Includes bibliographical references and index.
ISBN 978-1-4758-0083-8 (pbk. : alk. paper) -- ISBN 978-1-4758-0084-5 (electronic)
1. Holistic education. I. Williams, Ellen, 1944- II. Title.
LC990.M38 2012
370.11--dc23

2012025944

The paper used in this publication meets the minimum requirements of American National Standard for Information Sciences Permanence of Paper for Printed Library Materials, ANSI/NISO Z39.48-1992.

Printed in the United States of America

Table of Contents

Introduction

The Foundations of Holistic Education

This book is built upon the assumption that education is at its best—healthiest and most engaging—when it is holistic.

By holistic education, we mean that the various dimensions of the teacher and student are honored and nurtured in educational settings and processes. Although there are several major ways in holistic theory to categorize the various dimensions of the individual, in this book we have used the following rubrics to discuss them: 1) organic, 2) psychodynamic, 3) affiliative, 4) procedural, and 5) existential. Any truly humane theory and practice of education must, we contend, celebrate and cultivate these facets of the student and teacher.

For, as holistic theorists argue, if an aspect of an individual's complete systemic functioning is ignored or abused, it will become ill, and that illness will spread and affect the other parts of the system. As in traditional Chinese medicine, holistic educational theory contends that health results from balance among all the parts of an organism. When there is too much of one and too little of another, some sort of pathology is inevitable over time.

For instance, when a child in a classroom is forced a large part of the day into the very narrow cognitive focus of memorizing data in order to perform well on high-stakes standardized tests, the rest of her system—her physical, emotional, cultural, and spiritual nature—will suffer from neglect and grow ill. She may well then begin to "act out" in class and at home. Soon, she will be diagnosed with a "learning disability" or an "attention deficit disorder" and pumped with chemicals in order to control her "medical" problem.

Sometimes there is, in fact, a medical problem in the child that needs attention. The authors, however (one of whom, in addition to being a professor of education, is also a psychotherapist) believe that in the vast majority of cases, it is not the student who is really ill but the educational system itself that is out of balance—pathological and pathologizing.

And not only students but also teachers can become "ill" in such a system. Teachers are people who generally feel "called" to their profession out of a deep concern for young people and a passion for their subject-matter. However, when they are forced to do little more than deliver pre-arranged, impersonal, and therefore joyless lessons to students to prepare them for anxiety-producing, high-stakes, one-shot standardized tests, they become bitter and burn out. Fifty percent of all teachers leave the profession within five years.

The best antidote to these maladies of alienation and discouragement in the classroom is holism. Each chapter of this book, therefore, deals with one of the five dimensions of healthy human functioning and suggests why and how teachers can attend to these dimensions in their students and in themselves.

Chapter 1, "The Organic Dimension," discusses the educational significance of the fact that the student is an embodied being—a physical organism. From conception to death, who we are is unavoidably involved with the fact that we are physical creatures. We are organic creatures who are moving through the world by means of our senses. Any view of education that does not recognize and accommodate this fact is necessarily incomplete.

Chapter 2, "The Psychodynamic Dimension," looks at the fact (so often ignored in educational theory and practice) that both the teacher and student are complex emotional beings, and that those emotions not only operate in the classroom but sometimes operate with a peculiar intensity there. If handled well, emotions profoundly enrich the classroom setting and give it life. If not handled well, they can disturb and derail even the most skillfully designed curriculum.

In "The Affiliative Dimension," chapter 3, we examine the cultural nature of teaching and learning. This is a matter of great importance in the twenty-first century, which has already been called "The Age of Multiculturalism."

What teaching and learning mean in one culture may differ (sometimes greatly) from what they mean in another culture—both in terms of how teachers and students are expected to relate to each other in educational settings and also in terms of what counts as important "knowledge," how to arrive at that knowledge, and what to do with it. We discuss these issues and offer some guidelines for how a teacher can create classrooms that are multiculturally vibrant, where everyone is learning from everyone else's perspectives on topics and activities in the classroom and all are arriving at higher and better places together than any one of them could have done individually.

Chapter 4, "The Procedural Dimension," builds upon the notion of the student as a "cognitive apprentice" in a classroom. Here the teacher, a sort of "master cognitive artisan," helps the student learn the specific procedures and discourses of the standard academic disciplines. This prepares the student—at a level that is consistent with his age and developmental capacities, of course—to "think" like a mathematician, historian, chemist, or psychologist, or what have you, and to do so in exciting conversation with the teacher and fellow students in the classroom as "a community of inquiry."

Chapter 5 covers "The Existential Domain." Here we look at the teacher and student as beings who are earnestly engaged in the ongoing life-project of finding, or making, meaning in their lives. This chapter discusses how a teacher can help students create narratives of empowerment and hope in their lives, just as she is always in the business of creating such a narrative for her life. When this happens in the classroom, then education has risen to its full potential.

As teacher educators, we have written this book for both practicing teachers and those who are still in preparation in colleges of education. The first part of each chapter, written by Cliff, is largely theoretical but also down-to-earth and (we hope) intuitively resonant to the reader. The second part of each chapter, written by Ellen, offers a wide range of suggested classroom activities in each domain from a veteran teacher, a principal in the public schools for over several decades, and a professor of education.

To avoid sexist language, we have alternated between "he" and "she" as the general pronominal referent from chapter to chapter.

Chapter One

The Organic Dimension

We are embodied. Each of us is an incarnation of a unique spirit that has taken on a specific form of flesh and blood. From conception to death, who we are is unavoidably involved with the fact that we are physical creatures.

However high our thoughts and aspirations may rise, however "spiritual" we may believe ourselves to be or hope we may become, we cannot ignore (or at least we *should* not ignore) the fundamental fact that we are organic creatures who are moving through the world by means of our senses. Any view of education that claims to some sort of human adequacy but that does not recognize and honor this reality is necessarily incomplete and must, in one way or another, crash into and be shattered by the intractable fact of the student's physicality.

In our faith tradition, it is believed that one's soul is an imperishable union of the physical and the spiritual. There is nothing spiritual that does not have some sort of corporeal component, and nothing corporeal is without a spiritual aspect.

If these things are true, then overlooking them is disastrous because doing so deprives spirit of a physical component while also trivializing physicality by stripping it of spiritual significance. Education that does not attend to the student's status as an organic being—with organic needs, problems and potentials—is therefore existentially incomplete and pedagogically lacking.

This is not a new idea. At the dawn of the Western tradition, Plato's vision of schooling in *The Republic* had all students taking part in varied and vibrant physical activities, which, beginning in the student's earliest school years, would serve the developing individual throughout his life (Plato, 1991).

Seventeen centuries later, the Moravian educator and scientist Jan Comenius also insisted on the importance of the physical dimensions of educa-

1

tion, leading to a multi-sensory pedagogy. "The sense of hearing should always be conjoined with that of sight, and the tongue should be trained in combination with the hand" (in Broudy & Palmer, 1965, p. 120).

One hundred fifty years after Comenius, the Swiss pedagogue Johann Pestallozi insisted that a child learned best where there was sensory engagement with objects, and the result was what he called "object lessons." What was learned in these object lessons would form the organic groundwork for subsequent cognitive and emotional growth in later years (Broudy & Palmer, 1965).

At about the same time, Friedrich Froebel, father of the Kindergarten movement, was also approaching education from a broadly integrative point of view that fully honored the student as an organic creation.

Froebel pictured the cosmos as a series of nested realities, each intricately interwoven with the others enclosing it. What this holistic cosmology entailed pedagogically was the idea that the student would not only learn *about* all the spheres of his existence but that, whenever possible, he would learn *in* them, too.

There was no such thing as a lesson that was only about the physical realm, for the physical realm was shot through with metaphysical import; and even the most abstract ideas or theories might have physical implications and consequences that needed to be acknowledged, and sometimes even experienced, in order to be fully appreciated (Broudy & Palmer, 1965).

This awareness of the organic realm in educating the student was a key feature of the more liberal, child-centered Progressive pedagogies in the late nineteenth and early twentieth centuries, especially in the American Kindergarten movement of Francis W. Parker. Kindergarten, of course, is a time in the child's life when a special premium is placed on the student's rapidly developing body. However, many liberal Progressive pedagogues were also vociferous about the need to attend to the physical dimension of education for adolescents and adults.

Chief among them was John Dewey (Cremin, 1964). "The map is not a substitute for personal experience," Dewey proclaimed in his 1902 classic *The Child and the Curriculum*. "The logically formulated material of a science or branch of learning . . . is no substitute for the having of individual experiences. The mathematical formula for a falling body does not take the place of personal contact and immediate individual experience with the falling thing (Dewey, 1904). Simply giving the student "logically formulated material" to read and lectures to listen to would, Dewey believed, always be an inferior way of teaching if not accompanied by real tasks for students to do, individually and together, that engaged the emotions and body as well as the mind.

In another book (Mayes, 2003) the lead author related a personal experience that has made this point real to him in a special way over the years.

Cliff never did particularly well in science in elementary or secondary school, but one of his most memorable lessons was a sixth-grade demonstration of the speed of sound. Mr. Mascari, his teacher, had been talking about how the speed of sound was much slower than the speed of light. Here was another boring and irrelevant fact for Cliff to remember, and one which was not only uninteresting but downright counterintuitive! How could light be faster than sound? When you turned on the TV, didn't the picture and the sound reach you at the same time?

Mr. Mascari took the class to the baseball field. With a track-and-field starting gun, he stood at home plate. The students all stood in center field. The teacher had given one of the girls in the class a stopwatch and told her to start the watch when she saw the plume of smoke come out of the barrel of the gun and stop it when she actually heard the shot.

Cliff will never forget seeing the plume of smoke issue from the muzzle but not hearing the loud rap of the gun until a heartbeat later. A whole world of teaching happened in that brief second between heartbeats. Light *was* faster than sound! Cliff knew it because he had *experienced* it—with his ears, eyes, and even nose because of the acrid smell of the smoke.

When the students later calculated the speed of sound by using the data they had collected on the baseball field, it was simply logical confirmation of what was already physically and psychologically real for each student. To *see* and *hear* the speed of sound lagging behind the speed of light had allowed each one to internalize that fact and thus to make it his own as something real, proximate, and subjectively potent.

For Cliff then, and even today, the idea of "the speed of sound" is invested with the hues of that Fall afternoon in the Arizona desert, with the smell of the browning grass of his elementary school's baseball field, with the sight of the curling and ascending smoke, and, moreover, by an aura of sensory immediacy that a mere concept could never have.

Perhaps the heyday of interest in the organic nature of the learner in American public education was in the 1960s and 1970s, when principled concern for and deep care of the organic realm of existence was a central feature of the countercultural movement of the time. Ecological awareness, more openness about sexuality, the exploration of alternative forms of medicine, greater care paid to nutrition, the practice of spiritually-oriented physical disciplines such as Tai Chi and yoga, the rise of bodywork such as Rolfing and Hakomi therapy—these all typified a waxing awareness of the body.

The ethos of the time was permeated by the notion that we ignored the organic nature of our individual and collective lives at our personal, political, and planetary peril. Educational theory and practice during this period reflected this sentiment as is evident in the titles of such works as "Education and the Body" (Schutz, 1976) and "A Curriculum for Feeling and Being" (Hendricks & Fadiman, 1976).

Now more than ever perhaps, education should take scrupulous care of the student's senses, which have been rightly called "a neglected dimension of education" (Sardello & Sanders, 1999). In a world in which children's experiences are ever more relentlessly mediated by the latest in technological inventions—which seem to appear on the market almost every day with mind- and sense-numbing speed—"the senses, and therefore perceptions and experiences, are disrupted and will continue to be disrupted by the stimulated world of technology, science, and economic pursuits." Not only children but all of us increasingly need "to become trained in the art of living in our senses" (pp. 226–27). This is a domain of education that has traditionally been handled in physical education classes.

However, with the ever stricter focus on getting students to garner higher scores on standardized tests, our youth are being allowed less and less time on the playground, in the gymnasium, or on the track, football, or soccer field; and many are being given virtually no time or opportunity—either while at school or home—to simply wander around in nature and learn the one-thousand-and-one incalculably rich lessons that such free-and-easy rambling in God's creation offers.

Indeed, even recreation for the postmodern youth largely revolves around a soul-paralyzing array of technological games. What Gardner has identified as two of the eight crucial intelligences—naturalistic and kinesthetic—get short shrift at best in most current educational programs.

Although it has reached a terrible zenith in the twenty-first century, the program to corporatize education and turn teachers and students into cogs in "the military-industrial-educational complex" has been ongoing since at least the closing decades of the nineteenth century and the early years of the twentieth century as education has come more and more to mirror and service the voracious needs of the metastasizing corporate state (Cremin, 1988).

There are many theories which both historical and sociological scholarship puts forward in its attempts to make sense out of this trend toward what the nineteenth-century sociologist Max Weber called the technical rationalization of societies since the Industrial Revolution and the rise of the nation-state in nineteenth-century Europe.

However, we believe that an even deeper cause than political or economic ones for this neglect of the senses in education has to do with our psychodynamic depths, and it involves the gendered nature of our experience, which oscillates—both within the individual and between individuals—between the twin poles of the archetypally masculine and archetypally feminine principles. What do we mean by the word "archetype"? As will often be the case throughout this book, let us turn to the psychological theories of the Swiss psychiatrist Carl Gustav Jung (1875–1963) to clarify this point (Jung, 1960).

According to Jung, an archetype is a basic structural element of the human psyche, one that is more ancient and that lies much deeper than one's merely personal subconscious. An archetype is a fundamental "lens" at the very core of our psychospiritual being, through which we experience and interpret the world. And since there are many "lenses" through which we view the world, there are, by definition, many archetypes that "filter" our experience in this primary, and even primal, way. Simply by virtue of the fact that we are human beings, we are born with these structures in our psychospiritual makeup and they largely determine how we see and understand things.

Archetypes manifest themselves in different visible forms in different historical periods and cultures. These are the wonderfully varied *archetypal images* across history and culture. But the archetypes themselves are fundamentally the same in all times and places, all individuals and groups. It is impossible to say how many archetypes there are. They may not even be "countable" since they may be very fluid, merging into and emerging from each other in an unconscious "energic" ballet of ongoing psychospiritual metamorphoses at our deepest depths.

Whether the archetypal structure of the human psyche is fixed or fluid, however, there are some very common archetypes. For example, let us look at the archetypal hero's journey.

All cultures have stories of heroes and heroines, deserts and forests of travail that the hero or heroine must pass through, ogres and dragons and devils that they must face, wise old men and wise old women who help them on their way, mysterious dwellings where they stay in the course of their journeys as well as castles that are either resplendent or menacing, kings and queens, priests and priestesses, tricksters and helpers, and, in short, all the other characters and places and objects that make up the mythic realm of our existence where some of our most enchanting or horrifying stories are told, and where the keys to the mystery of our existence reside.

These are examples of archetypes. They are predispositions that we all have (undoubtedly from birth but perhaps maturing over the course of one's lifetime) to make sense out of what it means to be a human being.

Since this primary realm of our psychological and spiritual nature lies deeper than merely the forgotten or repressed elements of our personal subconscious (which Freud studied), Jung called it the *collective unconscious*—*collective* because it belongs to all of us, inheres in all of us; and *unconscious* because it exists at much deeper levels than the merely individual subconscious. One's personal subconscious might be pictured as that part of the "boat" of our existence that floats under the surface of the ocean, our conscious ego being the boat itself that we purposefully and practically guide through daily social reality. But the collective unconscious is the eternal ocean itself that surrounds us, and its currents, waves, and eddies are the indeterminate number of fluid and ultimately inscrutable archetypes that *are* the infrastructure of our psychospiritual dynamics.

Two or the most powerful archetypes are the Great Father and the Great Mother—or the eternally masculine and feminine principles. [1]

The Great Father is concerned with measurement, analysis, systematicity, and their practical manifestations in the forms of various tools and technologies, both concrete and abstract.

The Great Mother, on the other hand, is concerned with intuition, art, natural processes, interrelatedness, and their practical realization as acts of nurturance and deep organic creativity. As the child-bearer and the one who, every month, experiences the biological reality of creative flow, the Great Mother is sensitively attuned to physical reality as something to be tended to, loved, and helped to unfold into full-bodied life. It is no coincidence that we speak of Mother Earth, for the earth, in her fecundity, *is* feminine. It is also no coincidence that etymologically the words "mother" and "matter" stem from the same hypothesized root word, *mater,* in prehistoric Indo-European.

The neglect of the physical dimensions of education is, the authors believe, the result of dishonoring the archetype of the Great Mother, casting her to the margins of our psyches and societies, especially in highly industrialized cultures. This alienation of the Great Mother is a core cause of the fact that teachers and students are growing increasingly bored, anxious, aimless, and depressed in classrooms. Where the focus is almost exclusively on the archetypally masculine with its devotion to analytical processes and its insistence upon quantitatively measurable results, the Great Father is exercising excessive sway at the expense of the Great Mother.

In other words, we suffer in the highly industrialized nations from a radical and pathological imbalance of the male and female principles. In naturopathic medicine and ancient Chinese philosophy, this imbalance of the masculine and feminine principles is seen as the cause of illness and evil. This is one of the great promises of multiculturalism in education in which a wide range of cultural perspectives are honored. For, indigenous First World cultures are often more in touch with the Great Mother than the so-called advanced nations.

With the growing obsession on higher standardized test scores in the service of corporate profitability, there is decreasing attention being given to the archetypally feminine purposes and goals of education.

Instead of being a space where teachers can help students deal with basic physical and emotional issues (both the physical and the emotional domains being very much under the sway of the Great Mother) at an organically healthy and developmentally appropriate pace, the classroom is becoming a patriarchal prison. Students are increasingly forced to gain information and master cognitive tasks as quickly as possible.

The consequences of this preoccupation with high scores on norm-referenced tests are grim, resulting in what some public health officials are calling "the new morbidity" among children.

> In the United States. . .the number of children with a diagnosis of attention deficit disorder (ADD) . . . combined with hyperactivity is growing rapidly. The drug Ritalin is often being prescribed for such children. Statistics vary but range from 1 million to 1.5 million children in the United States now receiving Ritalin. . . . Whereas some children genuinely need help because of constitutional problems in the nervous system, many others appear to need help primarily because they cannot accommodate to current educational practices. (Almon, 1999, p. 254)

This excessive use of Ritalin, Concerta, and later-generation drugs that are designed to tighten cognitive focus and diminish the need for physical activity in young people is symptomatic of a pathology that is not finally in the children but in the system itself.

For where the categorical demands of the Great Father are not humanized by the tender nurturance of the Great Mother, there is literally hell to pay—and it is a price of admission into many classrooms (especially public school classrooms) that our teachers and children are increasingly being compelled to pay; and, in the case of the children, they are being drugged into submission when they do not or cannot do so.

This is nothing less than socially sanctioned child abuse. It is a grave ethical problem. Clearly, any pedagogy that aims at completeness, balance, and health must honor the student (and teacher) as embodied beings. If their needs and potentials are not recognized or fostered at this level, then, as in any system, the part that is neglected will either atrophy and die—spreading its post-mortem toxicity throughout the entire system—or will find a way to make its needs known by undermining the functioning of the other parts of the system.

At any rate, in holistic theory, not to attend to some part of the total system is to breed a local pathology in that system that will ultimately pollute or pillage the rest of the system (Wilber, 2000).

Speaking of the organic bases of communication, the great curriculum theorist James Macdonald noted a distinction between "disembodied intellect" and "sensori-motor presence" in the classroom:

> In everyday life communication in its cultural context is a complete organismic response involving facial gesture, bodily posture, emotional mood, tacit understanding, and personal organic needs. The activity of school in contradistinction focuses almost entirely upon formal structures of communication, primarily language. Thus, the curriculum goals are essentially divorced from the concrete biology of the student. . . . This divorcement of the verbal from affect and psychomotor activity. . .helps teach students to distrust their own

values, emotions, and bodies as basic aspects of life and to this extent dimin-
ishes the full meaning of being alive. (Macdonald, 1995, p. 124).

Foshay (2000, p. 45) has very practically suggested that physical education
should permeate the entire curriculum. With his following seven criteria for
good physical education in mind, teachers and school leaders may better
attend to their students' awareness of and care for themselves as physical
beings:

> 1. Physical growth—changes in the body that accompany increasing age; 2.
> health—prevention of physical disorders; 3. body image—awareness of the
> bodily organs and functions, awareness of one's appearance; 4. movement—
> including sports and dance; 5. body language—nonverbal expressiveness; 6.
> metaphors deriving from primarily physical experience; 7. image schemata,
> including path, cycle, blockage, and so forth.

Cliff has discovered in his career as a psychotherapist what a crucial role
physicality often plays in an individual's deep transformation in therapeutic
processes. And what, after all, is education at its best other than profound
change into ever more humane and skillful forms of seeing, being, and acting
in and on the world?

Education is not therapy but, as we will see in the next chapter, it inevitably has either healthy or unhealthy psychological consequences for the student.

It is possible to talk through and around an issue with a client in therapy
from every possible angle until there is simply nothing left to say or analyze
about it. Still, the person may not change, or may not change enough. Why is
this?

Often it is because there is a physical component to the issue—a sort of
musculoskeletal infrastructure to it—that keeps on debilitating the person in
spite of the fact that he has a firm cognitive grasp on the problem.

A searing tightness around the heart, a sickly feeling of dread in the
limbs, shortness of breath, dizziness, or dull waves of weariness—all of these
sensations and many more may continue to distress and debilitate the individual in spite of the fact (and sometimes precisely *because* of the fact) that
he has an exhaustive intellectual understanding of what is going on with him
but has not addressed what his system has registered in the past and is now
ingrained at an organic level regarding the problem. These things can only be
dealt with through various forms of body work.

One of the most damaging and damning aspects of the current obsession
with testing and technology in American education is that it conditions a
student to live almost exclusively in a mental world divorced from any other
aspect of the student's being. As the student receives the message—test after
test, class after class, year after year—that all that really matters is scoring

well on a standardized test and winning institutional praise and (later) financial rewards for doing so, that person becomes increasingly divorced from his body.

The result of such alienation from one's organic nature is usually some form of neurosis, and sometimes even psychosis. The danger of "de-organicized" education, in other words, is that it works to neuroticize the individual, who must then be "treated" by drugs brought to us by the same corporate structure that created the problem in the first place.

As in therapy so in education: If we are to touch people in intellectually, emotionally, and ethically enriching ways, we must understand that there is a physical substratum to almost every human experience. Indeed, it is difficult to think of any human experience that is not intertwined with—and even enabled by—the fact that the person who is having the experience is an embodied being. There are many fine books that offer a wide array of specific ideas and activities regarding the organic dimension of education (Hendricks & Fadiman, 1976; Whitmore, 1986).

If education is to be liberating for a student, and not simply a means of perpetuating vicious or vapid social practices and arrangements, it must resist the program of our governing corporate power structure to make us cogs in the machine. With its increasingly powerful tools and techniques of standardization, surveillance, and consumerism, the corporate state and transnational corporate capitalism are more and more erasing the individual, depriving him of unique experiences.

They largely accomplish this by in a sense depriving the individual of his own unique, even idiosyncratic, experiences. This is done by deluging the individual with words, images, and constructs that define the nature and delimit the horizons of how he sees interprets, and values his world. As in Orwell's prophetic novel, *1984*, with its idea of "Newspeak," these terms and constructs are largely provided by the corporate elites, slickly packaged by the media, and subtly instilled in the individual by the various institutions in which he is obliged to perform.

By dangling before the consumer ever more seductive media that, as their name implies, "mediate" the individual's experiences through so many layers of electronic "filters," *im*-mediate and deeply personal experiences are becoming an endangered species. More and more, *to have* an experience—one that is uniquely one's own—is, in itself, a revolutionary act.

And since, as the branch of philosophy called phenomenology (which is the study of the nature of experience) shows, one's experiences are inseparable from one's senses, education that helps a student engage healthily and authentically with his senses will be liberating, while education that does not do so will tend a student not only ill but also unfree. For, "what if," as the sociologist Brian Fay asks, "oppression leaves its traces not just in people's minds, but in their muscles and skeletons as well?" (1987, p. 146). If this is true, then attending to the sensory domain is not only good pedagogy; it is politically and ethically imperative.

It is largely this nurturance of the student as a delicate and beautiful physical organism that distinguishes such alternative schools as the Waldorf schools from traditional education. Even in dealing with such abstractions as numbers, the Waldorf educator takes an organic and psychologically rich approach to introducing children to the world of math.

> First graders live in a world of imaginative pictures; they have a natural feeling for the archetypes implicit in the world of numbers. . .The number one, for instance, represents more than a digit. It can be thought of as the largest number, for it contains all other numbers within it. The number two, in contrast, denotes duality, contrast, opposites. The children in first grade might encounter some of these dualities in stories which contrast a bright, sunny day and dark, gloomy night, or a mighty king and the queen who rules with him. With the number three comes a dynamic quality, with four a quality of stability and form. There are four seasons, four directions, four elements. . .A student who has gone through this process will never again consider a number simply as an abstraction or merely as a mark upon a page. (Trostli, 1991, pp. 343–44)

Knitting, dancing, painting, modeling clay, and caring for animals on the school farm also make knowledge tangible in ways that rarely happen at traditional schools. Such things should be a feature of public classrooms as well.

We teach and learn best when teaching and learning are pleasurable. Therefore, let true, deep, and abiding joy characterize the tenor of our educational acts.

APPLICATION: THE ORGANIC DIMENSION

Through the ages philosophers, theoreticians, and educators have believed in the importance of giving students first-hand experiences in learning. Plato, Pestallozi, John Dewey, and other greats have promoted the importance of designing learning activities that engage students' senses and involve them physically in mastering new skills and understanding abstract concepts. These organic experiences provide a wonderful foundation on which students can build understanding of essential learning outcomes from the concrete to the abstract. By attending to the organic dimension, teachers can make learning far more interesting and relevant, which in turn, will likely increase student learning.

KINDERGARTEN SOCK WALK: SCIENCE AND LANGUAGE ARTS

Studying the science of plants can be deadly boring and meaningless to students if it is limited to reading a chapter in a book and answering the questions at the end or completing vocabulary worksheets followed by a paper and pencil test. But science can be brought to life by combining it with language arts and giving students first hand experiences in doing science. One example of providing such learning experiences from the organic dimension is the Kindergarten sock walk.

This activity should take place in the fall after plants and weeds have dried up; it is most effective if each primary grade student is accompanied with a learning buddy from the upper grades. In a nearby field or area where plants have dried up, primary and intermediate grade students cover their shoes with old socks and walk through the field. As students move through the dried plants and weeds, seeds cling to their socks. At the conclusion of a five minute walk, students remove their socks and put them in a clean empty milk carton. Once back in the classroom, students plant their socks and, over the course of three to five weeks, watch them grow!

In a learning partnership, primary and intermediate grade teachers prepare their students for this joint experience. Students at each level study the germination and development of seeds into healthy plants during the science period and work on interpersonal skills of effective communication during the health period. Each primary grade student has an intermediate learning buddy. Buddies share learning experiences, such as viewing movies on seeds, exploring Internet sites, and reading books on plants. Primary grade students draw pictures of what they have learned and intermediate grade students produce a children's book on seeds using a combination of expository text, diagrams, and pictures.

Prior to the sock walk, primary students show intermediate grade buddies their pictures and retell books their teacher has read to them; intermediate grade students read the children's book on seeds they produced to their primary buddies. The unit is culminated when learning buddies walk through the field gathering seeds on their socks while engaging in conversations with one another. Teachers who have used the sock walk report that the relationships between the primary and intermediate grade learning buddies lasts throughout the school year.

THE WETLANDS PROJECT: SCIENCE AND SERVICE LEARNING

This organic learning activity is best done in partnership with representatives from an environmental agency that has responsibility for the wetlands area that is identified as the focus of the project. As part of an academic study of the wetlands—reading text, completing assignments, seeing demonstrations, hearing guest speakers, and interacting with each other around problems of the wetlands environment, students adopt an area that is at-risk. Under the guidance of their teacher(s), students establish a partnership with a representative of the environmental agency.

As the project is carried out, students visit the wetlands area, assess its condition, identify contributions they can feasibly give to help it become more viable, and make a plan for doing so. For example, two Utah teachers helped second through sixth grade students improve a wetland area along a river through the following activities:

1. Replant native plants
2. Clean the area along the river bank
3. Raise money to place signage beside the walkway along the river bank
4. Purchase benches

Organic learning projects could be carried out in many different venues and for various aspects of the environment.

NOTE

1. How much these two archetypes are biologically determined—that is, to what extent men tend to live in and identify with the archetype of the Great Father and women with the archetype of the Great Mother—is difficult to say, although there is some compelling evidence that the biological influence is profound and more determining than social conditioning. Nevertheless, it also seems to be true that social and familial factors play a role in how, and how much, a particular individual identifies with the masculine or feminine principles; and it also seems to be true that every individual is, to some degree, a mixture of both. See Anthony Stevens, 2000.

Chapter Two

The Psychodynamic Dimension

We are emotionally deep and complex beings. Waking or sleeping, we can hardly think a thought or experience an image that is not laden with emotion—from simple amusement or mild distaste to love, joy, fear, anger, or revulsion. Approaching education as if it were merely, or even primarily, a matter of learning facts and figures and how to reason (as important as such things undoubtedly are) overlooks the simple fact that what and how human beings know is almost always tied into how they feel about what they know—or what they *believe* they know.

Even a scientist in her laboratory has feelings about what she is studying. Unless she has been given dull work to do (in which case she is still *feeling* something—namely, boredom), she is probably studying something precisely because she is interested in it, perhaps even passionately interested in it.

And if the results of her study have an effect upon whether or not she is granted tenure, given more research money, or awarded a prestigious prize, she will probably be deeply invested emotionally in how her experiments turn out. She might, consciously or unconsciously, choose to attend to certain bits of data and overlook others in order to further her cause.

As the historian of science Thomas Kuhn has shown, the scientist with a revolutionary, paradigm-shifting idea often meets with massive resistance because that scientist's colleagues are so emotionally, professionally, culturally, and sometimes even financially invested in the "truth" of a certain model of reality that they all subscribe to that they are just incurably blind to the new reality—or the new aspects of reality—that the radically different model is revealing (Kuhn, 1970).

As the branch of learning theory called "conceptual change theory" has shown, cognition is not "cold." It is "hot" (Pintrich, Marx, & Boyle, 1993). Any idea is liable to being "heated up" by a countless variety of factors.

13

What one thinks (which often basically means how one feels) about every-thing from the American Civil War and abortion to the welfare-state or Hemingway's novels will be affected by one's personal experiences, family dynamics, socioeconomic status, cultural perspectives, ethical values, and overarching goals in life.

A quadratic equation is always a quadratic equation, of course, but how one feels about quadratic equations varies greatly from person to person. In the authors' and our parents' generations, for example, it was felt that women were not generally very well suited to doing math, leading to what was called "math anxiety" among women.

Despite the fact that women are undoubtedly just as capable of doing math as men are, many women would be filled with dread at even the sim-plest problems in algebra. And for some people from First Nation cultures, algebra may be an interesting curiosity but may also not tell them very much that is of interest to them about the cosmos as they see it. [1]

The *whole* student is involved in learning, not just her ability to concept-ualize, for her emotions and experience-colored imagination may well be in-volved in picturing "how to conceive a squared root, a declined verb, a balanced equation, the plural of 'deer'; or the harshness of the Arctic envi-ronment, or the nature of myth, or the varieties of human conflict regula-tion—or the meaning of infinity" (Jones, 1968, p. 82).

All of this is not to say that education must be steeped in emotionalism. It is to say, however, that it is difficult to imagine any aspect of a total educa-tional situation that does not involve emotions, sometimes very potent ones. The teacher who is unaware of or indifferent to this fact will often be an ineffective teacher because she is an insensitive one.

That teaching and learning are an "emotional experience" should not be surprising (Salzberger-Wittenberg, 1983). In one sense, our lives are an on-going series of teaching and learning situations. In the nursing room, the mother and child teach each other the primal protocols of nursing, and learn deep lessons about themselves and each other while doing so. At the moment of death, the dying person may serve as a teacher—her way of passing out of this realm of existence evidencing (in the silent witness of her last glance into one's eyes) what it means to have lived well, to die well, and whether some-thing might await us after our last heartbeat.

Situations need not be so dramatic to be educative.

Walking home from school with your arm around a friend, sharing the experience of winning or losing a big game with your team, a first kiss, discussing a dream with a confidante, doing something reckless with a col-lege buddy just for the sake of doing something reckless, landing a good job and getting to know the ins-and-outs of it, showing one's daughter how to ride a bike, objecting to an outrageous idea at a city hall meeting and then fielding the criticism you get, tending to your garden seriously for the first time after you retire, seeing your father's expression on the face of your grandson: these are just a tiny sample of those countless little moments and lessons that make up our lives and that constantly put us in the role of teacher or learner (and sometimes both at the same time) as we move from grade to grade through the larger schoolhouse of life itself.

To be a human being is to teach and learn. This principle is thoroughly woven into the fabric of our existence. How could teaching and learning—wherever and whatever the educational site—be anything but "emotional experiences"? To consider the emotional and even subconscious aspects of teaching and learning might easily cause the teacher to ask with some trepidation if she needs to be a therapist in order to be a good teacher. The answer to that question is a resounding "No!" Teachers are not therapists and students are not patients. It would be professionally and ethically wrong for the teacher to try to play therapist to her students.

However, given the fact that conscious and unconscious emotions and impulses are deeply implicated in virtually every act of teaching and learning, it is wise for the teacher to practice her craft with an abiding awareness of that fact—as well as with at least a basic knowledge of how the psyche operates so that both she and her students can find not only cognitive but also emotional excitement and growth in the classroom.

Armed with such knowledge, the teacher is much more likely to create classroom environments in which students are emotionally nurtured—not intimidated, anxious, aggressive, depressed, or any of the other generally unproductive feelings that students (and also teachers) may all too easily have in an emotionally unsupportive and inappropriate environment.

We can all think of at least one classroom in which we were stuck as students for a term or two where the teacher was emotionally maladroit, even hurtful, and we emerged from that experience with a bitter taste in our mouths and even an active dislike for a subject-matter that may have otherwise caught our imagination and spurred us on to further study.

In this manner, the teacher, although not a therapist, has considerable power to turn a classroom into a "therapeutic environment" in which students are emotionally enriched and therefore want to engage more deeply with the subject matter, or an "anti-therapeutic environment" in which students are emotionally ignored or perhaps even abused and therefore lose interest in an area of study that may have otherwise enlightened and empowered them.

Besides, no two students in a classroom will ever have the same experience of what is going on in the classroom. Student A's experience of what is being taught and how it is being taught and how other students are responding to all of this will never be exactly similar to Student B's, and it may even be radically different. These differences in how various students are *experiencing* the teaching-and-learning situation depend upon a wide variety of factors.

These factors range from things as all-encompassing as a given student's religious convictions (or lack of them) and relationship to authority-figures in her family life (which attitudes will often affect how she views the authority-figure of the teacher in the classroom) to how well the student slept the night before and what kind of breakfast she had.

Thus, in addition to the "official curriculum" (what the teacher has been told by the state that she must teach) and the "operational curriculum" (what she *actually* decides to teach in her classroom), there is also the "subjective curriculum"—which refers to the different ways that different students *experience* what is being taught. There are as many subjective curricula in the classroom as there are students.

It is easy to see, then, that although education is not therapy, educational processes will almost inevitably have therapeutic or anti-therapeutic, compelling or alienating, emotionally up-building or emotionally problematic effects on students. To be sure, we must never lose sight of the fact that one of the primary goals of formal education is to help students become more cognitively complex and technically capable in many areas of theoretical inquiry and practical application. This is what has been called "the mastery dimension" of education, and it is vital. However, equally crucial is "the therapeutic dimension" of education, which we will discuss in greater depth in this chapter (Shalem & Bensusan, 1999). Our argument is that these two dimensions of education go hand in hand. Students will master material all the more quickly if they are emotionally engaged in and strengthened by the process. They will grow more emotionally confident and whole as they experience more and more cognitive successes in the classroom.

If the heart and head are not allies in the classroom, they quickly become foes. The classroom then becomes a battleground, and teachers and students become the victims of an unnecessary conflict between thought and feeling, which, in the last analysis, can never be healthily separated in a human being.

In short, "learning is "neither 'cognitive' nor 'affective' but a compound of both" (Barford, 2002, p. 57). That place where cognition and emotion overlap is called "the imaginal domain" (Barford, 2002, p. 57). And as every teacher knows, students learn more quickly, internalize more deeply, and employ knowledge more creatively if they are learning for reasons that are personally meaningful and emotionally compelling to them—if, that is, they are learning because of what is called their "intrinsic motivation" to do so.

On the other hand, they learn less well, if they learn at all, if they are learning simply to gain artificial rewards or avoid externally applied punishment. These are merely "extrinsic motivations" and they do not produce very deep or durable results. It just makes good pedagogical sense for the teacher to understand these things and know how to work with them in order to promote intrinsic motivation among her students.

Thus, in the remainder of this chapter, we will offer a brief overview of several of the most important models of the psyche. This will lay the groundwork for a discussion of their relation to educational issues. We will then conclude with some suggested activities for both teachers and students that address this holistic domain.

A BRIEF OVERVIEW OF DEPTH PSYCHOLOGY[2]

It is generally believed that Sigmund Freud was the first person to systematically study how the psyche operates and that he was a psychological explorer who "discovered" the unconscious. But this is a fallacy. The complex operation of human emotions and their connection to the subconscious mind have been objects of systematic study and theorizing since at least the 1700s (Ellenberger, 1970). It was Freud, however, who scientifically systematized all of these findings and speculations into a model of the psyche.

Classical Psychoanalysis

Classical Freudian psychology has lost a great deal of popularity in recent decades because of what is correctly perceived to be its overemphasis on sexuality as the primary preoccupation of the subconscious mind and the overriding motivation for all human activity. Freud's one-sided and not very flattering view of the human being as just a very intelligent animal in constant search of sexual gratification or some symbolic substitute for it simply does not square with what most of us intuitively know—namely, that although sex is an important part of life, it is just one part of life and far from the whole picture.

We have many needs that range from the simple one to belong to groups of people who care for us, to the desire to do meaningful work in life, to the search to find a mate who will share life's journey with us, to the ethical impulse to discover for ourselves if there is a God and, if so, what our relation to that God should be. To reduce all of these aspects of the total human experience to mere sexuality is simplistic and leads to despair since it does not answer to either the breadth or height of our desires, tensions, and aspirations.

Still, Freud did provide important preliminary insights into some of the formal mechanisms of *how* the psyche functions and how it is structured even though his analysis of *why* it functions as it does was exaggeratedly sexual. In fact, to give Freud his due, we find, if we look closely at his writings, that as early as 1912 he had begun to move in the direction of what would later be called "ego psychology."

This is the school of depth psychology which holds that a person's primary psychological motivation is not sex but rather the fundamental human urge to develop a healthy sense of identity, a strong ego—one that is capable of loving, being loved, engaging in creative work, and being socially productive. Even Freud wrote that there were "various points in favor of the hypothesis of a primordial differentiation between sexual instincts and other instincts, ego instincts" although it is true that he put overwhelming emphasis on the sexual instinct (Freud, 1912/1957, p. 106).

Freud took the term *ego* from the Latin word for the first-person singular pronoun "I": *ego*. The ego is who "I" am in the world. It is not a static entity. It might be better pictured as the ongoing mental flux of memories, perspectives, dispositions, and capacities that make up one's conscious awareness of oneself and one's environment from moment to moment, situation to situation. The ego is that part of the psyche that enables an individual to realistically perceive and successfully navigate the natural and social worlds, which she must do in order to survive. The ego works in the service of what Freud called *the reality principle*.

When it is operating well, the ego is able to satisfy the reality principle by striking a functional balance between one's social roles and duties (these exist in the "upper tier" of the psyche that Freud called the *superego,* the site of all the moralistic, and sometimes excessively moralistic, demands we make on ourselves) and one's animalistic, mostly sexual desires (these exist in that "lower tier" of the psyche that he called the *id*, which knows nothing but *the pleasure principle* and the energy of *libido*).

In healthy individuals, the ego functions as a middle tier of consciousness. From that position, the ego is constantly negotiating agreements between the forces of the pleasure-seeking id and those of the socially demanding superego so that the individual can get some measure of pleasure but can do it in a socially productive and acceptable way.

The overall picture that finally emerged in the Freudian model, then, was of a three-layered psyche: the id (which was amoral and even immoral), the ego (which strove to follow *mores* and thus to be "moral" but also to get libidinal gratification) and the superego (which was unyieldingly "moral" and hypercritical). When these tensions—between the ego and the id, the id and superego, and the ego and the superego—could not be successfully managed, they would be repressed.

Repression was not always successful, however, because repressed energy would sometimes press to the surface in the partial and painful form of *neurotic symptoms*—or what Freud called a *reaction formation*. When this happened, the person needed therapy.

In therapy, a patient would often project onto the therapist some of her core issues, often those that related to her relationship with her parents. This is not surprising since the therapist is also an authority figure—a kind of parental figure—and one, moreover, who is being given special access into very private regions of her psyche, where family-of-origin issues, images, and impulses still swirl with a mighty force. If the patient had a difficult relationship with her father, she might "see" in the therapist certain of her father's characteristics, especially the ones that were particularly difficult for her to deal with—whether or not the therapist actually has those characteristics.

This process of the patient projecting her relationship with important people from her past onto the therapist in the present can provide the therapist with useful information about issues that need to be dealt with in the course of therapy. Freud called this process *transference* since the patient was transferring things from her past onto the therapist. But transference is not a one-way street.

The therapist is not a god. He has his own psychodynamic issues. Hopefully, he has dealt with his issues at a deeper level than the patient has. But one never successfully resolves all of one's psychodynamic issues in this lifetime. They are too multifaceted and too profound to ever be completely mastered. Since therapy is such an emotionally potent and ethically high-stakes endeavor, the therapist can thus easily get caught up in the whirlwind of the process, too, and begin to project his issues back onto the patient.

This is called *counter-transference*, a term devised by Jung. Because of the inevitability of counter-transference in any deeply engaging and transformative therapeutic process, it is necessary that the therapist himself be engaged in a continual process of self-examination, self-analysis, in order to minimize counter-transferential projections onto the patient which may do the patient harm.

Generally speaking, however, the diametrically conflicting demands of the id and the superego did not require therapy and were more or less successfully resolved by a natural process that Freud called *sublimation.* In sublimation the psyche strategically allowed forbidden energy to express itself in a much reduced, highly symbolic, and therefore socially acceptable form. Thus the id would get some form of gratification while still adhering to social norms. Instead of playing with its own feces, for instance, the child would learn to shape figures in clay and might ultimately become an architect or sculptor. The infant who had been inadequately breastfed might sublimate the frustrated desire for the nipple into smoking cigarettes as an adult. And instead of physically uniting with his mother—the object of the famous Oedipus complex—the young boy would learn to sublimate that need into sexual desire for wife, thereby directing primal passions into the socially approved and socially cohesive vessel of marriage.

However, when sublimation failed—when the id's desires could not be adequately satisfied in socially acceptable ways—the psyche, if it was to prevent the person from literally acting out exactly what the id wanted, would have no alternative but to banish those desires from conscious awareness. This was the only way the individual could "go on" in the world without engaging in rape, murder, theft, or other socially unacceptable practices.

This painful and usually messy psychological process of violently shoving down and banishing desires from any kind of awareness or expression is what Freud called *repression.* The place to which repressed energies were banished Freud called the *subconscious.* The subconscious was thus a kind of garbage heap at the base of the psyche—or a dark prison-house that held all those horrible revelations into our brute nature that we must exile into black forgetfulness lest they overwhelm and destroy us.

Sadly but inevitably, repression was simply the price that the human animal had to pay in order to live harmoniously with others in society, for if everyone acted out on their animal urges the result would be chaos and bloodshed and the destruction of society, and this would spell extinction for one and all.

According to Freud, we are not only sexual animals. We are also social animals who rely on each other in order to survive. The human animal, therefore, had no choice: when sublimation failed, the individual had to curb her brute nature by repression if she were to live productively with her fellow beings in those social roles and according to those social rules that not only defined her life but that, indeed, made her very survival as a communal creature possible.

In the last phase of his writing and practice, Freud enlarged the notion of the id, or *libido,* considerably, calling it *Eros* and depicting it as a sort of generalized life-instinct within the individual (still deeply involved with sexuality but not completely reducible to it) which was constantly doing battle with a death-instinct that he called *Thanatos*—or the desire of every creature to return to an undifferentiated state of eternal rest in the primal ground of being. In this war, death must inevitably triumph for it always has the last word. "The goal of all life is death," Freud grimly concluded in *Beyond the Pleasure Principle*, for "the inanimate was there before the animate" (Freud, 1923/1957, p. 160).

Post-Freudian Theories

In this section, the focus is on three of the most important psychoanalytic theorists who followed Freud—Kohut, Winncott, and Fairbairn—because their thoughts have proven to be especially fertile for educational theory in the last several decades.[3]

Although their theories differ in many ways, these three post-Freudians have similar objections to classical Freudian psychology. The most important one is that they feel the basic psychological motivation is not sex but the need to enter into a relationship with a significant other or others in order to create and cultivate a sense of personal identity and existential wholeness.

Sex may figure into this need for relationship but is secondary to the primary need to relate to others as a potent and authentic "self" in the world—a "self" who, according to some neo-Freudians, finds final fulfillment in discovering ethical and spiritual meaning in life (Meissner, 1984; Rizzuto, 1979).

Heinz Kohut[4]

Heinz Kohut is the father of "self-psychology," in which the striving for a stable and holistic sense of self is primary. Sexual issues will certainly come into play in defining and maintaining a self, as will many other issues, but they will all be oriented to the core goal of self-definition and self-mainte-nance—what Kohut called a state of *healthy narcissism.*

The person who does not have such a relatively stable and unified sense of self suffers from a *narcissistic wound.* The foundations of a person's sense of self are formed by her earliest relationships with primary caregivers—or *selfobjects,* so called because they are the objects of the infant's earliest attention and affection through whom the infant learns about the world and itself (Kohut, 1978).

The selfobject is not, in the final analysis, actually the other person or thing that is helping an individual define herself but is the *image* of that person or thing that the infant (and later the adult) has internalized—or, in psychoanalytic parlance, has *introjected.* Put simply, the image that we carry around within us of an important person in our life usually corresponds only approximately to who and what that person really was—and sometimes may not really correspond at all.

Typically, the infant's central selfobject is its mother. The infant's psyche is so dramatically shaped by its interaction with its mother because it is symbiotically fused with her at this primal stage. Indeed, in the infant's earliest view, the mother is indistinguishable from itself, according to many developmental theorists.[5]

If the mother's interaction with the infant communicates love and accep-tance, the infant begins to assume that it is loveable and accepted, and that the world is essentially dependable and beneficent. The infant comes to see itself as essentially a good, stable, and integrated being. In short, the child's *primary narcissism* finds confirmation and gratification in its union with the loving mother, and it does so in two essential ways.

The first is in *the mirroring transference,* which consists of the infant seeing itself through the mirror of its mother's responses to it. The second is in *the idealizing transference,* in which the infant, enshrining the mother as not only the apex of reality but indeed as reality itself, finds its own ideals in its merger with this godly personage. The "idealized parental imago . . . is gazed at in awe, admired, looked up to, and [is that] which one wants to become" (Kohut, 1978, p. 430). The idealizing transference is the root of the child's ability to define, have, and maintain values (Eagle, 1993).

The opposite of this kind of value-instilling mother is the one who communicates to the infant in her interactions with it that she is unhappy that it has come into the world, unduly anxious about it, or repelled by it. This lays the foundation for a variety of psychic disorders in the developing infant and eventually in the adult—especially *the narcissistic personality disorders.*

For what the infant sees in the "mirror" of the mother is its own undesirability, inadequacy, and lack of unity. It thereby learns as well—in a colossal failure of the mirroring and idealizing transference—that the world is neither welcome nor welcoming but, rather, rejecting, cold, dangerous, and confusing, and that it is a place that is either valueless or that has values that are unattainable or irrelevant.

The narcissistic personality disorders are pathological attempts to experience the primary mirroring and idealizing that the person never experienced as an infant—or never experienced enough. These pathological manifestations are called *secondary narcissism.* Healthy human development thus originates in primary narcissism and concludes in healthy narcissism. When primary narcissistic needs are not met, the many dysfunctions of secondary narcissism result.

In his later work especially, Kohut's focus is on the relationship between healthy narcissism and productivity. He explores "the ways by which a number of complex and autonomous achievements of the mature personality [are] derived from transformations of narcissism—i.e., created by the ego's capacity to tame narcissistic cathexes [i.e., releases of psychic energy] and to employ them for its highest aims" (1978, p. 460). Humor, empathy, wisdom, and creativity are fruits of the positive transformation of primary narcissism into mature narcissism.

D.W. Winnicott

From the extraordinarily rich body of work of British child psychotherapist D. W. Winnicott, we will look at three concepts that have had significant educational implications: *holding environments, good-enough mothering,* and *transitional objects.*

Like Kohut, Winnicott sees the roots of psychic health or illness in the infant's relationship with its mother. Ideally, the mother will provide a good *holding environment* for the infant. This may actually involve the physical act of lovingly holding the infant. Yet even when it does not, it does entail the mother providing the child with a physical and emotional context that is appropriate to its needs and beneficial to its growth—an environment, in short, that *holds* the child so that the child can mature in safety.

A wide extension of "holding" allows this one term to describe all that a mother does in the physical care of her baby, even including putting the baby down when a moment has come for the impersonal experience of being held by suitable non-human materials. In giving consideration to these matters, it is necessary to postulate a state of the mother who is (temporarily) identified with her baby so that she knows without thinking about it more or less what the baby needs. She does this, in health, without losing her own identity. (Winnicott, 1988 [1969], p. 259)

Note Winnicott's insistence in the above passage that the mother should provide not only adequate holding for the child but also that she should do so "without losing her own identity." Good mothering does not mean *perfect* mothering in which the mother must always be available to the infant, meeting its every need almost before it arises.

A so-called perfect mother would have to forego her own identity, needs, and boundaries. Such *perfect* treatment of the infant, far from actually *being* perfect, is seriously flawed, for it does not allow the infant to experience those moments of opposition that are necessary for it to experience—in healthy and monitored doses, of course—so that it can begin to mature.

A mother who psychically fuses with her infant to such an extent that she completely forfeits her own healthy sense of boundaries will present to the infant an unhealthy example of what relationship means—namely, giving oneself over so completely to "the other" that one's self begins to disappear. When one's self begins to disappear, the result is anxiety, depression, and many other psychic ills.

On the other hand, *good-enough mothering* prevents burnout in the mother by providing for her own identity and even occasional mistakes. "Good-enough mothering gives opportunity for the steady development of personal processes in the baby"—processes that will feed positively upon the mother's realistic humanity and not her neurotic perfectionism (Winnicott, 1988 [1962], p. 456). Needless to say, such mothering is still fundamentally loving, careful, and adequate to the infant's physical and psychic development.

Good-enough mothering provides for the mother's increasing separateness from the child as it begins to mature—a process best embodied and symbolized in weaning. With increasing separation, the infant, and then the older child, comes to sense both physically and emotionally the existentially necessary lesson that there is a grand divide between the world of Me and Not-Me—the Not-Me world first presenting itself to the child's awareness in the form of the withdrawing and sometimes even absent mother. To negotiate the space between the world of Me and Not-Me, the infant will come to rely upon *transitional objects.* What is a transitional object?

To take a prime example: the infant's own thumb, which replaces the mother's breast when the infant wishes to nurse but mother is not available for feeding, is the first transitional object. The thumb, through a basic exercising of the infant's still primitive imagination, comes to replace the absent breast. The thumb is no longer just a thumb to the infant, although the child does not mistake it for a breast either; rather, the thumb becomes a transitional object—a psychologically living symbol that stands in place of the original desired object.

The significance and power of the transitional object lies in the fact that the child's imagination invests it with the power to satisfy at least some of its needs. In the same way, a favorite blanket becomes the child's substitute for the mother when she is away. Through creative fantasy, the child turns the blanket into a transitional object that is now not a blanket or a mother but a "poetic" fusion of both—an imaginative "transition" between both.

> The thumb stands for an external or NOT-ME object, is symbolical of it as we would say. The external object being sufficiently available, it can be used as substitute. This transition is itself allowed to take place slowly and gradually, in the infant's own time. Transitional objects [such as pieces of cloth, dolls, teddy-bears, toys, or what have you] are provided or are adopted which (when the infant is resting from the arduous process of sorting out the world and the self) are cuddled or pushed away without being classified as thumb or breast symbols. (Winnicott, 1988 [1954], p. 436)

As the child develops, it chooses more complex transitional objects to symbolically express and deal with the existential gap between its inner needs and outer realities. In a sense, therefore, *all of our philosophical and artistic products, our concepts and images, are highly evolved transitional objects through which we express our fundamental existential need to interpret and interact with external reality.* The transitional space is the place and the transitional object is the thing where the interior world of "I" and the exterior world of "Other" can come into fruitful contact.

Winnicott even goes so far as to suggest that culture is a collective transitional social object in which a group of people experience and express their shared experience of reality. The transitional object is that space that bridges inner and outer reality, the subjective and the objective, in the form of a fruitful symbol.

W.R.D. Fairbairn

Fairbairn's basic idea is that "libido is not pleasure-seeking but object-seeking" (Eagle, 1993, p. 75). *It is not primal drives that energize the psyche but the need to enter into human relationship.* "It must always be borne in mind. . . that it is not the libidinal attitude which determines the object-relationship but the object-relationship which determines the libidinal attitude" (Fairbairn, 1992 [1941], p. 34).

What is most interesting about this important theorist for our purposes as educationists is Fairbairn's insistence that over-intellectualization can represent "a general tendency on the part of individuals with a schizoid component to heap up their values in an inner world"—attempting thereby to avoid human relationship by creating a "substitute" for them.

Instead of actual relationships with other people in real world of emotional give-and-take, such individuals turn all their energy into the world of abstraction, in which they can get lost and hide from other human beings. Fairbairn is here talking about individuals who would almost always rather be buried in a book or sequestered in a lonely lab than be with other people. "This high libidinization of the thought process," wrote Fairbairn, is characteristic of people who "are often more inclined to develop intellectual systems of an elaborate kind than to develop emotional relations with others on a human basis"; indeed, such individuals are inclined "to make libidinal objects of the systems which they have created in lieu of the pleasure of human contact" (1940, p. 41). Intellectualization, "a very characteristic schizoid feature," can thus be misused as an

> extremely powerful defense technique [which often operates] as a very formidable resistance in psychoanalytical therapy. Intellectualization implies an overvaluation of the thought-processes; and this overvaluation of thought is related to the difficulty which the individual with a schizoid tendency experiences with making emotional contacts with other people. (Fairbairn, 1940, p. 20)

With this basic understanding of some of the major models and tools of depth psychology, let us now use them to gain a better understanding of the psychodynamic dimension of teaching and learning.

THE PSYCHODYNAMICS OF TEACHING AND LEARNING

The first, most general, and perhaps most important lesson that psychodynamic theory has for education is that a student's emotional and subconscious life will often be a factor in whether the student does or does not learn something. Those same factors may also affect the *degree* to which a student's concepts change about something. Conceptual change theory has demonstrated that a student's ideas about something may undergo anything from slight to total change under the influence of instruction.

For instance, a student may well have been taught in her school in Indonesia, a predominately Islamic country, that there were really no such things as concentration camps during the World War II in which over six million Jews died, and that stories about the camps are simply Zionist propaganda. Let us say that this student relocates with her family to the United States when she is fourteen.

For the next four years in her U.S. high school, she will learn in virtually every history class that the camps were real and the Nazi crimes there against not only Jews but also Catholics, homosexuals, and gypsies, who also died there, were heinous. Because of her previous education, however, and her family's ongoing belief in the nonexistence of the death camps in Europe during World War II, she might still wish to cling to their beliefs.

However, given the fact that she is presented every term with contrary evidence, she has to modify her opinion somewhat since the evidence of the camps having existed is so overwhelming. Thus, she might strike a sort of compromise, agreeing that there were death camps but probably only a few of them, that not many people died there, and that those who did die there somehow deserved to die anyway. To be sure, her conception of death camps will have changed under the course and force of instruction, but the change will have been quite slight. One of the ironies of anti-racist material in the schools is that students who come to the class with racist ideas often twist the messages of the anti-racist material in such a way as to reinforce their prejudices (Devine, 1995). Or, they may change their minds to a certain extent, beginning to believe after reading the anti-racist material that it is unfair to discriminate against people because of their race or ethnicity. However, those same students may not want to live in the same neighborhood with such people or want their children to intermarry with them.

In short, a student's ideas about something may change quickly or slowly, partially or completely, depending upon how heavily invested she is in the idea(s) under analysis. And this is true of all of us—not just of students in the classroom. We tend to learn life's lessons slowly, kicking and screaming along the way; for, change is hard and is not simply a matter of mere cognition but also of one's emotional, ethical, cultural, and spiritual commitments.

Certain so-called learning problems, therefore, are less a matter of the student's cognitive powers and more a matter of her complete identity. Just because a student does not "learn" something, or does not choose to learn it, or "learns" it in only a partial fashion, one cannot necessarily conclude that that student has a "learning disorder." She may have very good reasons *not* to accept something simply because an authority figure is telling her it is true.

Indeed, as the curriculum theorist George Counts proclaimed in the 1930s, teachers and students should all approach any official curriculum in a critical fashion since what counts as "important" and "true" knowledge in what the state wishes to teach may have been decided by people who have an interest—and sometimes not a very politically or ethically healthy one—in what teachers are "supposed" to teach and students are "supposed" to learn (Counts, 1932). One must never lose sight of the fact that students are—or should be—free agents who should be given increasing latitude as they grow in deciding for themselves what is true or false, relevant or irrelevant to them.

Any educational program that does not acknowledge, and indeed celebrate, this ethical fact is either merely a form of technical training (not transformative education) or an attempt to oppress both teachers and students by imposing pseudo-knowledge upon them in order to control them intellectually, emotionally, and politically. When that happens—as is too often the case in state-sponsored education today—then schooling ceases to be educative and becomes a miseducative means of indoctrinating the young into some form or other of totalitarianism. Attempting to extinguish authentic emotions in teaching and learning—which is the primary consequence, and we would also argue, the primary purpose of standardized education—is politically and ethically reprehensible. It not only does damage to the student's deep psychodynamic life but also renders her incapable of deep and complex thought. This leaves her ill-prepared her to be an enlightened citizen of a democracy. Hence, many psychodynamic theorists over the last century have argued that democracy depends in no small measure upon emotionally rich, balanced, and empowering classroom environments in our schools (Mayes, 2009).

EGO PSYCHOLOGY IN TEACHING AND LEARNING

Ego psychology—from its tentative roots in Freud to its elaboration in Kohut, Winnicott, and Fairbairn—has a great deal to offer pedagogical theory and practice. Above all is the idea that it is very difficult for someone to have a healthy ego if she never experiences success in learning.

A student who consistently fails at everything (or most things) that she tries to do in the classroom will have a hard time believing that she is, or ever could be, an efficacious and valuable person in the world at large. Such a person develops what is called a wounded "learning-ego," and this is a wound that may easily come to permeate her overall psychological health (Anthony, 1989). Put simply, a person who feels stupid is not bound to be someone who thinks much of herself in general.

Now, we are not arguing for artificially inflating a student's self-esteem with frothy and false happy-talk about how wonderful she is in every way and at every task! Such flattery simply sets the student up for even more painful failures down the line.

The primary function of the ego, it will be recalled, is to successfully negotiate the reality principle. Self-esteem and a healthy learning-ego must therefore be realistic. Otherwise, the person's artificially propped up learning-ego will inevitably crash into reality at some point or other (as John Adams said, "Facts are stubborn things") and will thus fail in its essential function. To be robust, self-esteem must be legitimately gained by the indi-

vidual—the result of actual successes that she has had as a learner who has
worked hard to master something.

What we *are* arguing is that every student is capable of attaining some
degree of mastery—small or great—in at least one field, and often various
fields, and the wise teacher knows how to identify and foster these potentials
in her students. Even in tasks where a student may not excel, or may not even
be very good, it is possible to break a difficult task for her down into meaningful and manageable units so that the student can do as much of it as
possible and can be appropriately acknowledged for her achievements, even
if they are small next to those of another student who is gifted in that particular area (Brophy, 1999).

In so doing, the teacher makes it much more likely that the student will
take pleasure in (or in psychoanalytic terms, *libidinize*) the tasks, topics, and
theories that make up that particular educational activity, and that the student
will grow emotionally in the process, not be stunted. The student's ego-
structure, strengthened by its newly found potency, experiences what is
called "effectance pleasure" (Wool, 1989).

Put simply, realistic empowerment breeds true joy. The teacher who is
sensitive to the psychodynamic nature of learning is better equipped to not
only teach a topic or academic discipline (the cognitive dimension of education) but to use that topic or discipline as a way of fostering emotional
growth and psychological heartiness in her students as well. Although not a
therapist, she is teaching therapeutically and transforming her educational
space into a "therapeutic classroom"—one that her students will look back
on with affection and gratitude, not bitterness and disappointment.

In Kohutian terms, then, the therapeutic classroom is one where students
may experience those "primary narcissistic" reinforcements that lead to the
emergence of a powerful yet compassionate ego—one that is secure in itself
and therefore does not need to prey on others out of the tragic hunger that
results from being "narcissistically wounded" (Kohut, 1978). In terms of
ego-psychology, students thereby become more liable to experience and enact that "courage to learn" and "courage to try" that is at the very heart of the
sane and efficacious ego—one that takes joy not only its ability to move
through life potently but in its ability to be of service to others on their
journeys as well (Cohler, 1989).

Moreover, without the courage to learn and to try, there is no creativity.
For, creativity always entails intellectual and moral risk, emotional exposure,
periods of doubt and drought, and frequent bouts of ambiguity. In short, it
requires courage. But courage is something that narcissistically wounded
students with their shaky learning egos generally have in very short supply.

Indeed, instead of being creative, narcissistically wounded students are
prone to two contrasting but equally disastrous psycho-educational pathologies: they either become neurotic overachievers in order to try to compensate

for their low self-esteem with the socially approved drug of high grades, or they refuse to try to learn at all because they are convinced that their best efforts will merely result in failure anyway.

Neurotic overachievement and dispirited underachievement—both of which grow like cancer under the toxic rays of standardized testing—provide paltry soil for the emergence of creativity in a student. It is individuals whose ego-structures are authentic and dynamic, and who therefore know both their talents and limitations, who can work, in health and humor, to generate ideas, engage in practices, and forge products that are individually and socially creative and restorative.

Kohut's idea of mirroring and idealizing transferences comes very much to bear in all of this. By being a self-aware, ethically mature, and intellectually open person herself, the teacher may mirror for the student—just as the mother does for the child—what the student's own potentials are, showing the student what she may become. This is the mirroring transference. And although the teacher is only mortal, her relationship to her students is such that she will have many opportunities in the educative spaces that she creates to examine, and sometimes even embody, various ideals for her students, who are thereby inspired to do the same within themselves, and in and for the world. This is the idealizing transference. As does the mother for the child, the teacher becomes a selfobject for the student in the evolution of her ego structure. And here a word of caution is in order. The ideals that the teacher is attempting to model for and inspire in her students must be humane, realistic, and realizable. They should not stem from the punishing, perfectionistic requirements of an overactive superego, whose heartless demands upon the student do not guide her into an ever deeper discovery and ethical uses of her efficacy but pound her into servile submission to artificial standards.[6]

In a similar vein, Kohut also warns that over-intellectualization (and perfectionism in general) is often symptomatic of a narcissistic personality disorder. This brings to mind Fairbairn's assertion that many people construct elaborate intellectual structures as a psychotic defense mechanism against authentic engagement (Cohler, 1989).

Indeed, Fairbairn's work is particularly enlightening in understanding the overachieving, hyper-intellectual student, for Fairbairn reminds us that in most cases "overvaluation of mental contents" is ultimately a desperate attempt "to heap up values in the inner world" to the exclusion of external reality, and therefore is symptomatic of an excessive libidinizing of thoughts and theories. The result in the student is often some form of "fanaticism" (Fairbairn, 1992 [1940], pp. 15–20).

And what is true for students in the schools is even more true for scholars in the university, where "'intensive inquiry' may in fact be pathological, and may lead us to consider carefully the degree of psychopathology incorporated in all research or intellectual work" (Hall 2002, p. 39). This is yet another example of how essential it is that cognition and emotion work together in order to balance and correct the excesses that each one, operating unchecked, is prone to fall into.

Winnicottian psychology also offers guidance in making and maintaining a therapeutic classroom. It will be recalled that Winnicott speaks of the need for the mother to provide a good "holding environment" for the child. Holding environments are spaces—literal and figurative—in which the child is safe enough to venture into new territory but protected enough that she will not wander so far away or into such dangerous areas that she could be seriously hurt.

The child will naturally experience minor forms of opposition as well as the occasional minor cut or bruise in her forays into unexplored regions. This is a good thing, for it teaches her how to meet, endure, and overcome those challenges that are necessary for growth and, in any case, are an inevitable part of life.

Similarly, the teacher may turn the classroom into a symbolic space where students feel free and able to venture out intellectually and emotionally into new conceptual and practical fields of thought and action. They will occasionally experience conceptual dead-ends, contradictions, and tension within themselves and with their fellow-travelers in the classroom in the course of this "imaginal exploration" into new cognitive and affective territory.

Far from being a problem, such things are desirable, for the student learns for herself the ins and outs of nuanced thought, frank and constructive discourse, and how to negotiate reality with her fellows. The classroom then becomes not only a lively holding environment but a "culture of learning" (Brown, Collins, & Duguid, 1988).

However, it is equally important that the teacher—like the "holding" mother in Winnicott's theory—"contain" the situation so that her students' forays into novel conceptual and emotional spaces do not go so far afield that the students land themselves and each other in blatant error, toxic passions, or unwise practices. To contain the learning situation, the teacher need not be perfect any more than a mother needs to be perfect.

Indeed, as Winnicott observes, it is not only the case that the mother (and the teacher) *cannot* be perfect (who can?); it is also the case that she *should not* strive to be perfect even if she could be, for that would consciously and subconsciously communicate to students the neurotic message that perfectionism is both possible and desirable. This would set the student up for all sorts of narcissistic wounds and unrealistic approaches to problem solving, which, to be creative, must allow for those moments of ambiguity and error that are part and parcel of the creative process.

In Freud's terms, perfectionism represents an unhealthy domination of the ego by the superego, paralyzing the ego in the fierce grip of superhuman demands that are beyond the child's and student's realistic ability. A fundamental problem in standardized testing is that it celebrates the "perfect" 100 percent score.

There is nothing more inimical to creativity than such perfectionism, where the student is caught in an exhausting race to perform flawlessly every time, and where what is "true" and "acceptable" is entirely defined by someone else. The problem with such standardized criteria is not just that they are artificial but that they represent the worldview of some other person, or groups of people, who are not necessarily wise or just. In corporate educational programs teachers and students are subordinated to someone else's political and economic agenda.

Thus, just as the best mother is a "good-enough mother," so the best teacher is a "good-enough teacher" (Wool, 1989). She accompanies her students as they roam through educational spaces where everyone—including the teacher—can experiment with ideas and emotions on "imaginal" terrain. On this terrain, students experience the vital but limited element of risk within an environment of fundamental safety.

In such an environment—an educative holding space—teachers, not needing to be "perfect," are much more likely to find their work exciting, and to communicate that excitement to their students, whose intellect and emotion are lighted to life by the flame of the teacher's passion. And students, not needing to be perfect, can take joy in learning, and thus can *truly* learn, not simply memorize. Good-enough teachers and good-enough students in an educative holding environment are fellow travelers over the endless imaginal landscapes of the curriculum.

In the liberated and liberating zone of such a classroom, the curriculum is not a static "thing" to be plodded through and tested on in order to see how well students can memorize concepts that are disconnected from each other and factoids that are dry as dust. Rather, the curriculum becomes a Winnicottian transitional object—something that the child grasps, appropriates, and internalizes in her own way as a transition—a bridge—between herself and the world.

The curriculum is most meaningful to both the teacher and the student when it serves this function—when, that is, it is an instrument that each can lay hold of in their ways in order to deepen and strengthen their relationship to their life-worlds. A curriculum that exists in and for itself alone is a static thing, inert. It is less a curriculum than a "cognitive object," the mastery of which does not involve learning but merely technical training.

There is a place for technical training, of course, but we must not confuse it with real education. Training merely *transmits* information to a student. It is a much lower-order pedagogical phenomenon than the profound intellectual and emotional *transformation* of a student—which alone deserves the dignity of the name of education. Perhaps the prime sin of corporate educational agendas is that schooling is turned into a way of enslaving minds into uncritical obedience through mere training. As a program of popular education, this is death to a democracy.

A democracy can thrive only when its citizens' minds and hearts have become acute and free in legitimate acts of true education—what the great pedagogical theorist Paulo Freire called education as consciousness-raising—which stands in stark opposition to the corporate program of institutional training as consciousness-numbing and dumbing down. As a static institutional object, the curriculum enchains teacher and student. As an imaginal transitional object, it is a path to freedom.

By drawing upon these insights provided by Kohut's, Fairbairn's, and Winnicott's ego-psychology, the teacher is much more likely to be able to provide her students with therapeutic learning spaces in which those students—emotionally tended to—they are able to experience maximum intellectual growth. Cognition and emotion, head and heart, work best when they work together, and rarely work at all when at odds. And they work to the student's disadvantage, even disaster, when they are not synergistically joined.

TRANSFERENCE, COUNTER-TRANSFERENCE, AND THE REFLECTIVE TEACHER

Common to all different schools of depth psychology is a recognition of the importance of transference and counter-transference. But transference does not only happen in the therapist's consulting room with her clients. Everyone tends to more or less project their needs, fears, and expectations onto others in those "attachments of daily life" that make up our everyday world (Stone, 1988, p. 273). And we all do so especially regarding authority figures such as political figures, policemen, commanding officers, physicians, bosses, and, of course, teachers. Individuals in positions of power tend to stimulate multivalent and passionate projections from us because they are, in a sense, "playing out" our original relationship with the first and most important authority figures in our lives—our parents. Most transferential dynamics reflect and reenact the primary projections that the infant and growing child made onto her parents (Cohen, 1988, p. 70). It is quite understandable, then, that the classroom should be a venue for transferences from students onto the teacher, for the teacher, like the parent, is guiding and shaping younger people in her charge who tend to look up to her.

Speaking of how teachers are transferential objects, the great Freudian psychiatrist of adolescence, August Aichhorn, wrote almost a century ago that

> we know that with a normal child the transference takes place of itself through the kindly efforts of the responsible adult. The teacher in his attitude repeats the situations long familiar to the child, and thereby evokes a parental relationship. He does not maintain this relationship at the same level, but continually deepens it as long as he is the parental substitute. (1990, p. 97)

For better or worse, the teacher is often the displaced object of the student's desires and antipathies regarding her own parents. If that child comes from a dysfunctional setting (and more and more of them do), it is all too likely that those hopes and fears may play out in the classroom in ways that may be problematic for both the student and the teacher.

The ten-year-old boy who has been psychologically beaten into submission by an alcoholic father may be unresponsive to the teacher if he is a male. Yet the same boy, emotionally enmeshed with a needy mother and overly sensitive to her neurotic needs, may be excessively tuned into a female teacher's slightest emotional shifts and may perform brilliantly in her class in order to satisfy her. These different attitudes in the boy may have little, if anything, to do with the quality of the teacher but a great deal to do with what the child is transferring onto his teachers.

Just knowing that such things happen in the classroom can be liberating for a teacher and can sometimes help her make sense out a student's puzzling responses to her. The teacher can be saved considerable grief understanding that a transference may be occurring in a situation where it would otherwise just be a mystery to her why a student is responding to her the way he is.

It is not necessary for a teacher to know the complex workings of transference as a therapist would, nor is it even necessary for her to know what particular issues a student may be projecting onto her, for her to find some real comfort in knowing that she is, in fact, not an inadequate teacher but a parental projection in the student's subconscious. This can save the teacher unnecessary irritation and confusion at a student's inexplicable behavior.

Of course, the teacher should not discount any problematic behavior by a student as "just transference." The teacher may be handling a learning situation clumsily, or may be counter-transferring her own deeper issues onto a particular student or group of students. For this reason, it is important that teachers engage from time to time in psychodynamic reflectivity upon themselves as teachers. This is a process of a teacher taking stock of her own emotional life in the classroom.

As we have seen throughout this chapter, the classroom is a particularly potent psychodynamic zone where the possibility and intensity of transference and counter-transference runs high. Psychodynamic teacher reflectivity can tap into these potent energies in the classroom so that the teacher can use them skillfully, not be derailed by them. It does this in two ways: first, it helps the teacher become psychologically clear about her own issues regarding teaching—especially power issues—so that he or she is less likely to act out on these issues in the classroom. Second, it offers the teacher tools for building on her psychological strengths so as to enrich her classroom practice.

By thinking in deep, personal, and systematic ways about the psychological foundations of her practice as a teacher, the teacher is able to bring her implicit—and sometimes unconscious—assumptions about teaching to light. Examples of questions that a teacher engaging in reflectivity might ask herself, are: *What psychological dynamics (i.e., personal needs, hurts, hopes, potencies, and fears) were involved in my decision to become a teacher in the first place? (How) are these dynamics and needs getting addressed and expressed in my classroom? Are they changing as I develop as a teacher? Is my development as a teacher affecting* them*? Are they benefiting me and my students—or are they ever destructive or inappropriate?*

Slightly different examples of questions at the personal level that have a more explicitly "pedagogical" ring, are: *How have my own experiences as a student shaped my images and models of good and bad teaching? Are these images and models empowering for me as a teacher or limiting? If they are positive, how can I cultivate them? If they are limiting, how can I eliminate them or harness them to better serve me and my students?*[7]

The psychodynamically reflective teacher, rich in self-knowledge, is well prepared to turn her pedagogical space into a therapeutic space as well—one in which she and her students thrive intellectually and emotionally in their shared imaginal journey toward greater light and truth.

OTHER IDEAS REGARDING THE AFFECTIVE DOMAIN OF EDUCATION

Grossman (1995) has outlined for teachers a wide variety of pedagogical strategies for enhancing the student's sense of self-worth and efficacy.

Grossman encourages the teacher to: 1) offer individualized instruction whenever possible; 2) help the student see the strengths that he brings to a task; 3) help the student be more accepting of his cultural style when it conflicts with mainstream expectations; 4) provide the student with opportunities to succeed in his strong areas; 5) encourage him to replace negative self-talk with positive self-talk; 6) break difficult tasks down into manageable steps; 7) demonstrate trust and faith in the student; 8) let students make choices about tasks and approaches when and as appropriate; 9) give dependent students help only when they truly need it; and 10) ask the student what he thinks about his work rather than the teacher always volunteering his own evaluation of it.

These suggestions are quite similar to those offered by Bandura (1986) in his ideas regarding how to enhance a student's "Self-Efficacy Perceptions." According to Bandura, a teacher can do this by: 1) helping the student set specific and difficult but attainable goals for himself; 2) modeling effective strategies for the student for solving the problem at hand; 3) providing the student with positive feedback and avoiding negative feedback; and 4) making statements to the student that help him see himself as a competent person who can make progress, even at a task that he may not be exceptionally good at (see also Shawaker & Dembo, 1996).

Many of these suggestions for practicing a positive pedagogy are nicely captured in Ames's easily remembered TARGET program, where each letter stands for an aspect of this pedagogy.

T stands for the fact that a teacher should select tasks that provide optimal challenge and excitement for students. *A* refers to authority. The teacher is in control but he negotiates ideas, tasks, standards, and prospects with students as much as is possible. *R* is recognition. Teachers should remember to give recognition to all students who progress, not just high achievers. Indeed, a child who is only performing at an "average" level with respect to a certain task may have had to exert a great deal more effort and integrity in reaching that level than a student who can excel with virtually no effort at all.

With the letter *G*, Ames is talking about grouping—capitalizing on Vygotsky's idea of the Zone of Proximal Development to promote learning and empowerment in all students through cooperative learning situations that minimize competition. *E* is about evaluation. Use multiple criteria in evaluating students, not just one or a battery of standardized tests, and make the tests as individualized as possible, allowing students to draw upon various types of intelligences and talents in order to offer a holistic "portfolio" of their performance.

Finally, *T* stands for Ames' advice to use time creatively, not just rigidly in utter slavishness to the clock and a prearranged lesson plan, but to "go with the flow" when the class is on to an idea or activity that is generating palpable collective interest, even passion. Be flexible. (In Brophy, 1997)

All of the above suggestions for conceptualizing and implementing a positive pedagogy of possibility for students will be enlivening and enriching for all students, helping them overcome whatever patterns of "learned helplessness" that they have fallen into for personal and/or social causes.

As Carol Dweck (1999) has so wisely reminded all teachers, a pedagogy of possibility can work miracles in helping turn children's images of themselves from "helpless victims" into "capable learners," who: 1) do not become upset by failure; 2) do not talk about the failure as a failure but as an occasion to regroup and redouble effort; 3) learn to devise new self-instructions and strategies in the course of facing a problem; and 4) recall past successes whenever they run into a snag and use those memories to realistically anticipate the possibility of future successes.

PSYCHODYNAMIC THEORY APPLIED

Winnicott (1969) described a growth-promoting holding environment for infants as both challenging and supportive. Kegan (1982) extended the holding environment to the growth and development of human beings across their life span. A healthy mixture of support and challenge provides the medium through which students engage successfully in the difficult work of learning and applying new knowledge and skills. Teachers provide support by knowing their students and designing learning experiences that are aligned with the ways they make sense of new concepts and skills. Teachers provide challenge by scaffolding students' learning on the upper levels of their competence by designing increasingly difficult learning tasks that deepen their thinking and extend their knowledge and skills (Kegan, 2000).

Teachers can increase student learning by helping them reflect individually and collectively on their own development. Student self-reflection is even more powerful when essential learning standards are translated into student-friendly language. Through these reflective processes, teachers facilitate students' understanding of themselves as learners, and empower them to take charge of their own learning in intelligent and productive ways. Following are practical ways teachers can use reflection to empower students to be confident in and take charge of their own learning and psychodynamic development.

REFLECTIVE DIALOGUE

In a safe holding environment, teachers provide a balance of support and challenge to help students take the risk of moving out of the comfort zone of known knowledge and skills to master more difficult concepts and skills. Stiggins, Arter, Chappuis, and Chappuis (2004) found that when teachers used the iterative process below (see figure 2.1) with their students, learning was three times more likely to increase than by reducing class size. This iterative process begins with helping students know where they are going or, put another way, providing them with a clear understanding of what they need to know and be able to do as articulated in essential learning standards.

At the outset of instruction, teachers present the targeted learning standard in language students understand and then give effective first-time instruction on that standard. Following initial instruction, teachers administer formative assessments and use that data to differentiate instruction. Using the assessment data, teachers hold reflective conversations with struggling students (Black, 2001) to show them know where they currently are in relationship to mastering the learning standard and to co-develop a strategy to close the gap.

This iterative process will be illustrated with the work of Alyson, a second-grade teacher who had targeted place value as the essential learning standard. At the outset of instruction, Alyson introduced the concept and explained to her students what they had to learn and be able to do to achieve mastery. She provided effective first-time instruction followed by a formative assessment. Alyson used data from the formative assessment to further differentiate instruction that addressed the range of learning levels.

Alyson engaged students who scored significantly below mastery in a reflective discussion around their formative assessment data. This process was designed to empower students to take charge of their own learning by showing them where they were in relationship to mastering the standard, to communicate her support, and to help them set a goal and make a plan to close the gap. Following is an actual dialogue Alyson held with Jody, who had scored 20 percent on the assessment with 80 percent required for mastery:

**2. Know where
they are now**

**3. Know how to
close the gap**

**1. Know where
they are going
(essential
standard)**

Figure 2.1

Alyson: *Jody, you scored 20 percent on the place value assessment and you needed to get 80 percent of your problems correct in order to achieve mastery. What are you going to do about it and how can I help you?*

Jody: *I can work harder.*

Alyson: Great! *Here are some ways in which you could work harder. You could complete extra homework at home, participate in the reteaching sessions, pay really close attention in the reteach class. . . . Which of these options would best help you master place value?*

Jody: *I will complete extra homework on place value, participate in the reteach class, and listen carefully to the teacher.*

Alyson: *Good. I will check your homework carefully and will be the teacher for the reteaching sessions on place value. I will pay close attention to your thinking and work, so I can make sure you understand the concepts in place value correctly.*

Jody: *Thank you.*

Alyson: *The next time you will be assessed on place value is at the end of the reteaching class. What score would you like to set as your goal?*

Jody: *I would like to try for 90 percent on the next place value assessment.*

Alyson: *Ninety percent is a wonderful goal. If we work hard together, you can achieve that goal!*

Jody did complete her extra homework assignments. She participated in the reteach class determined to master place value. She listened carefully during instruction and worked hard to complete assignments correctly. Alyson paid close attention to Jody's understanding and helped her on the aspects of place value that were confusing. On the final assessment, Jody scored 100 percent, exceeding her goal by 10 percent. What a celebration that must have been.

In this second-grade classroom, Jody's experience is not the exception, but the norm because Alyson has created a holding place for students that challenges them to accept responsibility for learning hard things and provides them with the right amount of support to succeed. Not only do Alyson's students achieve the essential mathematics standard but they develop power to take charge of their success. While understanding mathematics is important, helping students see themselves as capable able individuals will serve them well in every aspect of their lives.

STUDENT-FRIENDLY LEARNING TARGETS

Much has been written about the value of teachers using clearly articulated essential learning outcomes to design and assess instructional practices to improve learning for all students. Unfortunately, this process clarifies what is to be learned to teachers, but not necessarily to students. Recently, education researchers have recommended that not only should learning targets be clear to teachers, but they should also be clear to students. Stiggins and his colleagues (2004) recommended that teachers translate learning outcomes into student-friendly language.

Learning outcomes written for adults can be transformed into "I can" statements that are understandable for students. Once these learning outcomes are clear to students, teachers can help them reflect on their progress toward achieving them and develop a strategy for closing the gap. Two examples follow:

Example I:
Learning Target One in teacher language:
Students will compare and contrast elements of text.
Learning Target One in student-friendly language:
*I am learning to compare and contrast elements of a text. This means **I can** say how parts of a story are different and the same.*
Learning Target Two in teacher language:
Students will summarize text.
Learning Target Two in student-friendly language:
I am learning to summarize text. This means I can describe the important parts of what I read in my own words.

A fifth grade mathematics teacher had her students reflect of their learning each day. First she translated the essential learning standard into student-friendly language and then had her students reflect in writing on their progress toward mastering the standard. One day she shared with the authors a delightful reflection that one of her students had written after a particularly difficult lesson on subtracting with mixed number fractions, a complex and confusing process. On this day one student wrote that he was "halfway between knowing and not knowing" how to subtract mixed numbers with borrowing.

Because this student knew that he was halfway toward mastering this learning standard, he and his teacher could work together to identify the parts he understood and the parts with which he struggled and then develop a strategy for closing the gap (Stiggins et al., 2004; Black, 2001). By so doing, this student could learn with confidence and the teacher could support him with targeted assistance. Through this process, students develop clarity of purpose and are empowered to take charge of their learning.

DEVELOPING HABITS THAT SUPPORT INDEPENDENCE

Forlini, Williams, and Brinkman (2010) recommend that one way to help students develop into productive and independent learners is to have them self-reflect on developing habits and academic skills that support independence. Below is a chart that Forlini and his colleagues (2009, p. 43–44) recommend intermediate to secondary teachers use to help students shape themselves into independent learners through self-reflective processes.

The value of this self-reflective process can be greatly enhanced by intermittently engaging students in a dialogue individually or collectively around the criteria from figure 2.1 to identify their strengths and set goals to refine areas that need to be strengthened. Forlini and colleagues (2009, p. 43–44) recommend teachers use the following questions to facilitate this reflective process:

- Which of the Life Skills am I doing especially well?
- What is one thing I can do to keep this life-skill strong?
- What one Life Skill could I make stronger?
- What is one thing I can do to strengthen this Life Skill

REFLECTING ON READING EXPOSITORY BOOKS IN THE CONTENT AREA

Teachers can use the reflective process to help intermediate and secondary students develop proficiency in reading difficult texts in various content areas. First teachers explicitly teach reading strategies that will assist stu-

Name: _____ Class: _____ Date: _____

Student Self-Assessment of a Long-Term Project

	Poor	Avg.	Good	Excel
Academic Criteria				
Topic well-researched				
Broad range of resources used				
Information written in own words				
Multiple viewpoints represented				
Life Skills				
My efforts were focused				
My time was used wisely				
My work ethic was good				
I avoided distracting others				

dents to unlock difficult content-specific text. Next teachers provide guidance and opportunities for students to select specific reading strategies for particular texts. Finally, teachers scaffold opportunities for students to reflect individually and collectively on how well the strategies they selected worked. An example follows in which students reflect on strategies used before, during, and after reading a text.

Pre-reading reflection. The instruction to students might be as follows: Effective readers use processes before, during, and after reading challenging texts in order to maximize their understanding of the content (Ogle & Lang, 2007). Before embarking on the assigned reading, plan the strategies you will use before, during, and after you read the assigned text. In the second column, check the strategies you plan to use during each phase and in the third column, describe the reason you chose that strategy in terms of its strengths and suitableness for the type of text you are assigned to read.

Post-reading reflection. Instruction to students may be as follows: Reflect on the cluster of strategies you used to glean essential understandings before, during, and after reading the assigned text. Suggested questions to ask yourself are:

1. What were the strengths of the strategies I used?

When I Am Reading to Learn Information from Challenging Textbooks

I. Before I read the textbook, I plan to. . .	Check Strategy	I chose this strategy because. . .
A. Use a preview protocol to identify the important parts		
B. Preview the questions		
C. Generate my own questions		
II. While reading the text, I. . .		
A. Made notes using a Y or 3-column diagram		
B. Created a graphic organizer		
C. Visualized ideas and thought of analogies		
D. Made marginal notes		
III. After reading the text, I. . .		
A. Wrote a personal summary		
B. Rehearsed and reconstructed concepts orally		
C. Asked and answered questions		
D. Connected the main ideas from this text to other texts I had read and/or my own firsthand experience		

2. What were the adaptations I had to make in order for these strategies to be useful to me?
3. If I were to read the assigned text again, how might I adapt the reading strategies I used or what different strategies might I select to increase my understanding of the material?

NOTES

1. Buddhist monk and psychotherapist Jack Kornfeld tells the story of chatting with the head monks one evening in the monastery where he was studying Theravada Buddhism in Southeast Asia. At one point, one of the head monks said something about how the sun revolves around the earth. Kornfeld, a well-educated Westerner, respectfully corrected his master, explaining how just the opposite was the case. After listening to Kornfeld's explanation, the old monk thanked Kornfeld for the explanation—but then added, with a wry smile, that, although it was interesting to now know that the earth revolved around the sun, such knowledge did not bring one any closer to enlightenment. See also Hewson, 1988.

2. The examination of depth and transpersonal psychology in this chapter is largely drawn from my article "The psychoanalytic view of education: 1922–2002." *Journal of Curriculum Studies*, 41(4). pp. 539-567., and from my book *Inside Education: Depth Psychology in Teaching and Learning* (2007), Atwood Publishing. I am grateful to Atwood Publishing and *The Journal of Curriculum Studies* for their permission to use that material in this chapter.

3. The reader who is interested in getting a solid overview of modern developments in psychoanalytic theory will find one in Eagle's (1993) *Recent Developments in Psychoanalysis: A Critical Evaluation.*

4. This section on the neo-Freudians first appeared in my book *Inside Education: Depth Psychology in Teaching and Learning*, and is reprinted with the kind permission of Atwood Publishing.

5. This idea has come under fire from some theorists who believe that the child has a sense of its mother as a distinct person, and not just an extension of herself, virtually from the first moments of conscious awareness (Wade, 1996).

6. The psychoanalytic educational scholar Ed Pajak pointed out to me several years ago how a student's overachievement may be the reflection of the needs of her narcissistically wounded parents, who vicariously get ego-gratification for themselves from their child's "stellar" performance in school. Such parents are attempting to prop up their own shaky egos by basking in the reflected glory of their academically high-performing child. This turns the child into a tool for satisfying her parents' unmet psychic needs. At best, this is psychologically unhealthy for a child, and at worst it is emotionally abusive of her—a sad and probably very common example of what Alan Block has called "education as the practice of social violence against children."

7. See the first author's books *Jung and Education: Elements of an Archetypal Pedagogy* (2005) and *Inside Education: Depth Psychology in Teaching and Learning* (2007) for more on teacher reflectivity.

Chapter Three

The Affiliative Dimension

We are cultural beings. We cannot be adequately understood apart from the cultures and subcultures that have molded us throughout our lives. Inevitably, each of us, although a unique being, is also embedded in a culture—and usually in various cultures.

Some of those cultures are a matter of birth. As one of the authors, Cliff, reports: "My mother was Jewish, my father was largely Italian, and both were second-generation Americans, born in New York City, in the early decades of the twentieth century—and into quite different economic circumstances, too, my mother from a well-to-do family and my father from a poor one. These were genetic, ethnic, social, and historical circumstances over which they had no control but which deeply impressed who they were.

"The product of their union, I carry all of those influences within me, too, in myriad ways that ceaselessly impact how I interpret the world and carry on in it. And then of course, there are the specific cultural circumstances surrounding my own growing up years. I was born in the American Southwest and lived in a poor neighborhood in the Tucson desert in the 1950s nestled between the Papago Indian Reservation one mile south of my house and the 'Chicano' barrios several miles to the north.

I came of age in the tumultuous 1960s in a household where my father was very conservative politically and my mother quite liberal. In virtually everything I say, see, and do in the course of the day, I can, if I stop for a moment and reflect on it, find strands of all of these cultural influences—and more—that make up the tapestry of my existence at that particular moment.

During that moment of reflection, I believe that I can isolate a core essence that is something that I am, uniquely, but I must admit that I find it difficult, and often impossible, to thoroughly separate that essence from all the cultural admixtures that are part and parcel of my 'identity' in this world."

There is nothing unique about Cliff in this. Each one of us is a multicultural "site." How each of us sees the world and acts in it and upon it simply cannot be neatly separated from our ethnicity, class, gender, nationality, socioeconomic circumstances, geographical location, historical circumstances, and a considerable list of other such cultural determinants. As conscious, self-reflective beings, we can engage in a process that the anthropologists George and Louise Spindler (1987) called "cultural reflectivity".

Cultural reflectivity refers to the process of bringing to awareness the various cultural forces that have contributed so greatly to the makeup and trajectory of one's life. One can bring these forces to consciousness to a considerable degree but never completely. For, one's cultures is so embedded within the individual, at the very foundations of the edifice of his awareness, that he could never dislodge all of those foundational elements and hold them up to scrutiny without undoing the edifice itself.

In other words, we can reflect on the cultural influences that make us up, and to some extent we can erase, modify, or replace them, but we can never do so completely. As Karl Marx wrote, "It is true that men make their own history. But they do not make it exactly as they please" (1852/2010, p. 1).

The twenty-first century has already been characterized as "The Age of Multiculturalism" (Fay, 2000). This is so for at least three reasons.

First, the individual in the highly industrialized countries has an ever increasing number of personal lifestyle options that he can select from in constructing a self-identity, a situation that is filled with both perils and possibilities. In these countries, the individual has a dizzying array of choices about how to construct—and periodically deconstruct and reconstruct—his personal identity. These ways of defining and redefining oneself *as* a self, and the freedom and resources to do so virtually at will, were not available—or even conceivable—in earlier centuries, and certainly not to the degree they are now (Giddens, 1991).

The foundation of this emphasis on the individual as a central—perhaps *the* central—philosophical, political, and religious fact of the human experience was laid during the fifteenth century, encompassed the sixteenth century, and spread throughout the seventeenth centuries in Europe during the course of the Renaissance. It was then systematized philosophically and published widely in the documents of the philosophers, economists, and political radicals of the Enlightenment eighteenth century.

In the nineteenth century, Romantic poetry gave artistic form to this celebration of the individual in his emotional depths and imaginative possibilities. And the rights of the individual were established as a political fact in the form of the new democratic nation-states that arose from the late eighteenth century on. What is more, the nature and status of the individual was arguably the most important philosophical issue of the twentieth century.

The twenty-first century is thus a historical continuation of and highpoint in Western culture's ongoing exploration into both the perils and possibilities of extreme freedom in the individual's constant (re)definition of himself (Giddens, 1991). Therapy, a relatively recent historical phenomenon in the last one hundred years, is simply one manifestation of the birth of the deep, complex, and dynamic "individual" who is constantly in the process of reflecting upon and changing himself.

Although we tend to think of culture as *collective* and therefore, in one sense, the very opposite of the individual, the historical ascendancy of the individual is a crucially important cultural phenomenon. It is the cultural focus of *Western culture* on the individual that has given birth to this proliferation of options in self-construction. Furthermore, the fact that one can make and remake himself over and over again means that *one may choose to belong to a shifting assortment of cultural and subcultural groups throughout the course of one's life.*

In addition to those groups that an individual is necessarily affiliated with by birth, in other words, there are also those groups with which he may affiliate as a matter of personal choice throughout his life span. The individual has become a composite site of increasing, and increasingly complex, cultural identities.

A second reason that the twenty-first century can be thought of as the Age of Multiculturalism is that throughout the twentieth century many of the so-called "grand historical and religious narratives" that have oriented the lives of so many people individually and collectively—telling them who they are and where they are going—have been contested and cast into doubt.

Consequently, individuals and groups find themselves either having to reassert their beliefs with a sometimes pugnacious fundamentalist fervor; or they must learn to coexist with others of different belief-systems—a difficult process at best, one requiring no small degree of imagination, creativity, and goodwill, and one that obliges individuals to reshape their belief systems so substantially that their forebears would probably not recognize the belief system as their own.

Third, the twenty-first century is the Age of Multiculturalism because endemic political conflict, new and inexpensive modes of traveling great distances, and the astronomical growth of the new communication technologies throughout the twentieth and into the twenty-first century have either weakened or broken down many national and ideological borders that previously defined people's lives geographically and ideologically but that are now increasingly "porous."

The result has been the felt need among many people whose cultures have been challenged and even ruptured to maintain their imperiled identity or reshape it—at the same time as they, along with everyone else today, are having to negotiate other cultural realities that are impacting their own with mounting speed and complexity in our increasingly interconnected global village.

Ours is indeed the multicultural century. As we will see in the second half of this chapter, this fact is very significant educationally. Before doing so, however, let us examine in more depth the idea of "culture."

CULTURES AND SUBCULTURES

Shade has offered a broad and simple but very useful definition of culture as

> a group's preferred way of perceiving, judging, and organizing the ideas, situations, and events they encounter in their daily lives. It represents the rules or guidelines a set of individuals who share a common history or geographical setting use to mediate their interaction with their environment. As such, culture might involve adherence to a specific religious orientation, use of a certain language or style of communication, as well as preferences for various expressive methods to represent their perceptions of the world, i.e., in art, music, or dance. Culture also determines the guidelines individuals within groups use to select the specific information to which they attend as well as the interpretation given to that information. (Shade, 1989, p. 9)

The sociologists Berger and Luckman provide a brief but handy list of the essential elements of any culture. According to them, cultures tend to have the following five characteristics:

> (1) there are some more or less universally shared assumptions among all the individuals; (2) individuals incorporate shared experiences of the social world in their individual biographies—that is, they tell the stories of their lives in terms, settings, roles, life stages, and ethical values that their culture provides; (3) a culture involves rules and roles—a body of transmitted "recipe knowledge" about how to act in certain situations; these are the parameters regarding when, how, and why one should behave as one does in various settings; (4) individuals internalize more or less the same elements of their shared social world; and (5) individuals share a language. (Berger & Luckman, 1967, p. 63ff).

Both of these definitions of culture turn upon the fact that a culture provides ways for seeing the world, being in it, and acting upon it. Culture strongly influences what we value, why we value it, and what we feel obliged to do—and not do—on the basis of those values. Both definitions also speak to the pivotal issue of language in the formation and maintenance of a culture. We will take up the issue of language presently. Let us first turn our attention to the question of values since it figures so prominently in the cultural dimension of education.

Culture and Values

The view that there are no, or few, universal values and that all, or most, of our values are generated by and specific to the culture in which we live, is called *cultural relativism.* Although not exactly the same thing as moral relativism, cultural relativism is often used as the basis for the argument that all morality is relative, that all values are culture-specific, and that no values can be defensibly adjudged as better than any others. This is the extreme "nurture" pole of the famous "nature" or "nurture" dichotomy. On this side of the dichotomy it is argued that what we think and do are basically shaped by external stimuli throughout our lives.

Epistemologically, this "nurture" position is grounded in the Lockeian view that consciousness is entirely determined by external conditions, which is why cultural relativism is also sometimes called *cultural determinism.* Cultural relativism as a school of thought is a product of cultural anthropology as an academic discipline, which arose in the late nineteenth and early twentieth centuries. Philosophically, it goes back to the Greek Sophists, who argued that morality was situational and, ultimately, a human construct, not part of some universal order or the result of divine injunction.

The opposing position—the "nature" pole of the dichotomy—is that we all carry within us a natural predisposition to find certain ideas and actions morally praiseworthy and others morally wrong. This is related to the Kantian idea of "categorical imperatives." According to Kant, we all know (simply by consulting our intuition) that certain things are morally praiseworthy, even obligatory. This intuition, and the morality it reveals, is, according to Kant, common to all people.

In the Western tradition, this view traces back to various roots, among them the Platonic idea of ethical and metaphysical absolutes, the Judaic Decalogue, and Christ's Sermon on the Mount. This radically "a-cultural" view of the source and force of ethical standards is the *innatist* position, for it holds that a sense of morality is innate in the human creature and not at all—or only loosely—related to cultural factors.

The authors of this book locate themselves somewhere in the middle of the continuum between cultural relativism and innatism.

On one hand, it seems to us to be beyond any shadow of doubt that culture dramatically influences how one interprets and acts upon the world.

On the other hand, we also believe, along with the mythologist Sir James Frazer, the cultural anthropologist Levi-Strauss, and the psychologist Carl Jung—three of the most important psychosocial theorists of the twentieth century—that we are all born with certain ethical and spiritual impulses, needs, and goals that are relatively constant across cultures (Frazer, 1935; Jung, 1978; Levi-Strauss, 1987). They have been variously called mythical motifs, structural cores, or archetypes. But by whatever name they go, they are innate in the individual—while at the same time being affected by the individual's culture.

But whether one takes a strict cultural determinist view of values, a radical innatist view, or lands somewhere in the middle, there are various things that we can say about culture and value that come very much to bear on a wide variety of educational issues.

First, whatever their origin, there do seem to be certain ethical standards that span cultures: the importance of honesty, the need for some form of sexual morality, the existence of rites of transition into adulthood, the importance of marriage and family, the necessity of social systems and duly appointed agents to enforce the law, the need to engage in socially meaningful work, and ceremonies that mark the end of one's life as a worker and parent and the beginning of one's status as a wise elder.

Anthropology has identified other cultural universals—such as the existence of art, dancing, bodily adornment, games, gift-giving, joking, and rules of hygiene (Giddens, 1991, p. 46). Perhaps most important of all the commonalities among cultures is that they offer the individual ways of understanding himself in a cosmic context—ways that typically involve systems of worship in that culture, ways that help one make sense of one's life, and ways that help the individual come to grips with the fact of death and the possibility of life beyond death. Indeed,

> Every human society is, in the last resort, men banded together in the face of death. The power of religion depends, in the last resort, upon the credibility of the banners it puts in the hands of men as they stand before death, or more accurately, as they walk, inevitably, toward it. (Berger, 1967, p. 52)

Furthermore, a culture organizes itself around its *normative values*. These are the generally (although not necessarily unanimously) agreed upon set of criteria that the culture uses to determine what kinds of attitudes and behaviors are strictly required; what kinds are acceptable within a range of more or less typical choices; what kinds are merely "tolerated" because, although "strange," they do not fundamentally rupture social order and are therefore allowable; and finally, what kinds of attitudes and behaviors are intolerable and forbidden because these attitudes and behaviors are seen by mainstream culture as so fundamentally injurious to its cultural foundations that they would threaten the very existence of the culture if they were condoned.

These standards—which are at the heart of a culture's legal and ethical systems—are the criteria for establishing and preserving the "average expectable" or "normal" way of seeing, being, and acting in the world according to that culture (Williams, 1987). They also offer justifications for and ways of coping with destabilizing forms of "deviance," usually with the goal of punishing a person for having violated the standards and, often, convincing or compelling the person to return to normative thought and behavior—"consensual reality" as it is called (Foucault, 1979).

The means of dealing with an individual or group of individuals who are thought to be violating norms beyond the point of tolerability exist at any and every level of social interaction: interpersonal, familial, institutional, and legal—and may involve the use of what the political philosopher John Locke identified centuries ago as the culture's "instruments of terror" (Locke, 1952). Indeed, as we saw in the previous chapter, a culture's normative values are also internalized as the person's superego, where they are heard as "the voice of conscience."

A culture's normative values typically exist in the form of a hierarchy— some being more central to a culture's definition of itself, some less so. Interestingly, these values do not begin in the form of clearly and rationally articulated ethical maxims or legal principles. Those systematic formulations come later. Rather, a culture's values begin in that culture's *sacred stories.*

These foundational narratives (a culture's originating myths) are the infrastructure around which a culture forms. Sometimes these foundational stories go back to the misty beginnings of recorded history—and sometimes go further back, leaping the gap into pre-historical, even cosmic origins— "once upon a time," *in illud tempus*, that sacred time beyond time when mythical heroes founded the culture and, by their words and deeds, defined its ideals (Eliade, 1974).

A culture's founding stories often trace the journeys and travails of culture heroes and heroines, who are often half human, half divine, as they confront a wide range of challenges. Their attitudes, actions, and apotheoses in the face of these challenges exemplify for the original members of the culture what is good and what is bad. After time, those notions of good and bad become formalized, sometimes written down, and in this way a legal system arises.

Far from being merely outlandish stories, then (as we have come more and more to see them in our unimaginative, literalistic, and rootless times) a culture's originating myths are moral example that lie at the very core of a culture and thereby serve as a primary mode of education into the culture's virtues (See also Bruner, 1996).

It has been argued that most culture's values are built around five basic sets of issues.

1. *Power distance* refers to the degree to which the less powerful members of the society agree upon and accept the fact that power is distrib-

uted unequally. The opposite poles here would be a strict monarchy as opposed to a radically pluralistic democracy.

2. *Tolerance of ambiguity* is a measure of how comfortable or uncomfortable members of a culture are in unstructured situations, how much a society accepts the unknown and how much it tries to control it.

3. *Individualism/collectivism* represents the poles in the balance that a society chooses to strike between the requirement that individuals take care of themselves versus integrating into groups. It is also refers to the degree to which the individual primarily sees himself in self-defined terms or in terms provided by his major social reference groups.

4. *Masculinity/femininity* refers to the width of the divide between gender-based roles, the degree to which biological differences are expected to be reflected in social and emotional roles.

5. *Long-term/short-term orientation* is the extent to which members of a society are expected to be able to accept delayed gratification of material, social, and emotional needs; persistence and thrift are examples of long-term orientation (Hofstede, in Mayes, 2007).

Another way of looking at how culture maintains its value system(s) is by considering how a culture *enables* the individual in certain ways and *constrains* him in others.

First, culture enables a person or group by providing necessary resources—and constrains them by *not* providing such resources, either because the resources are simply not available or because they are denied to certain groups (while often being provided to more favored groups). Second, culture delimits the range of a person's or group's available options by rewards (sometimes extravagant ones) and punishments (sometimes draconian ones) and thereby defines the horizon of that person's or group's possibilities.

Third, culture mediates action by determining—sometimes overtly, sometimes much more subtly—if and how various groups are allowed to interact with and impact each other. Fourth, culture determines much about the individual's concrete and social reality simply by the fact that it gives the names and defines the purposes of objects and the roles of people (Fay, 2000).

Subculture

Within a culture there are various *subcultures*—and typically an increasing number of them as a culture becomes more structurally and ideologically differentiated. As noted above, a major reason that our day and age is both rife with problems and overflowing with possibilities for the individual is that he has—at least in the highly industrialized liberal democracies—a plethora of subcultural groups to identify with, and thus a plethora of ways to define himself as a complex of unique subcultural combinations—ways that he can, and increasingly does, change or reconfigure with increasing ease and speed.

How one "constitutes" oneself in this environment of proliferating options is what the British sociologist Anthony Giddens has called one's "life-style politics"—including everything from one's religious affiliations and deeply held political convictions to one's taste in clothing, music, and food (1991).

Other common subcultural criteria are gender, what geographical part of the culture one comes from, the dialect one speaks of the culture's central language (if the culture has a central language, as most do), one's ethnicity if the culture is multiethnic (and postindustrial cultures almost invariably are in the twenty-first century), sexual orientation, marital status, socioeconomic class and work experience, and recreational interests.

There are also subcultural identifications that revolve around one's age, involving shared historical memories that members of a generational cohort have had. For instance, members of the authors' generational cohort might ask each other "Where were you when Kennedy was assassinated?" while members of a later generational cohort pose the dramatic question "Where were you on 9/11?" Generational cohorts tend to share certain characteristics and preferences that provide foundations for subcultural formations and identifications (Arredondo et al., 1996).

Additive Multiculturalism and Cross-Cultural Communication

If the twenty-first century is indeed the Age of Multiculturalism, then one of this century's most important tasks is to learn to deal intelligently and sensitively with diversity so that it becomes an advantage, not a disadvantage. In other words, we need to take what is called an "additive" view of diversity, not a "subtractive" one.

We live in a time when instruments of mass destruction are becoming easier to build or obtain, and even easier to conceal and transport. Furthermore, social and technological systems in our century are becoming so stunningly complex and interdependent that undermining them requires only that one node in the network be destroyed to cause serious disruption in the entire network, even system-wide failure.

In such a tenuous and high-stakes world as this, it is matter of enormous political and ethical importance that we find ways to build upon diversity in order to enrich our lives individually and collectively through this diversity, not be torn apart into irreconcilable and aggressive factions because of it. What are some ways to facilitate communication across (sub)cultures?

One way—which applies at almost every level, from the global to the national to the local, and right down to the classroom level—is to employ what Fay has termed "The Principle of Charity" and "The Principle of Humanity" (Fay, 2000).

According to the Principle of Charity we should "count others like us unless there is clear reason not to." We must train ourselves to see beyond surface difference in order to identify and build upon our common humanity—our shared hopes and fears, loves and aversions. We are, after all, *all* human beings.

According to the Principle of Humanity, we should "count others intelligible in their own terms unless there is clear reason not to." Despite our fundamental similarity as human beings, there *are* substantial differences across cultures in worldviews and practices, and the Principle of Humanity helps us know what to do in the face of such differences. It requires that our first line of response be to take a generous view of the differences, assuming that they serve the members of the other culture—making their existences richer in their own terms, investing their lives with a salutary sense of meaning. This we must do unless "there is clear reason not to."

And in that last phrase is implicit, again, the Kantian idea that there are certain ethical universals—the violation of which is so egregious that it goes beyond the limits of tolerance. These universals provide the "clear reasons not to" condone certain practices in other cultures. For, some (sub)cultural practices—such as ethnic cleansing, spousal abuse, child abuse (including child pornography and child prostitution), and torture, just to name some of the most obvious ones—are so fundamentally repugnant to any humane sensibility that they must be rejected outright.

Of course, the difficulty lies in determining what to make of cases that are possibly less dramatic than the ones just mentioned but are still deeply problematic. In these instances, where is the line to be drawn between what is questionable but tolerable and what is unquestionably intolerable? Understanding both the importance as well as the limits of tolerance is one of the most pressing political and ethical demands of our time.

Key to understanding and building upon (sub)cultural differences is the ability to communicate cross-culturally. This is a necessary skill for teachers to have in the multicultural U.S. classroom, where increasing numbers of students are coming from, and adhere to the norms of, (sub)cultures other than the white middle-class culture whose assumptions and whose very language tend to define the "official" culture of most classrooms, setting the standards for "correct behavior" and overall "success" in those classroom.

For everyone, but especially for people like teachers who work in concentrated multicultural venues, it is imperative to grasp some of the basics of intercultural communication. A first step in doing so is to appreciate the difference between a cultural *boundary* and *border*.

A (sub)cultural boundary refers to "the presence of some kind of cultural difference" between two groups, A and B (Erickson, 2001, p. 40). If these differences are approached in a constructive manner in which each culture legitimately honors the other and both are willing to learn from each other, with neither attempting to lord it over the other culture, then an "additive" spirit prevails. This is key to fertile cross-cultural communication, for there is no ethically rich communication when one of the communicative partners is attempting to dominate the other one. This is as true at the cultural level as it is at the dyadic level in, say, a conversation between life-partners. If communication is to be a tool of liberation of self and other, there must be respect between the dialogical partners and a willingness to being shaped by each other—to some degree, at least. Otherwise, "communication" functions not really as an existentially legitimate "exchange" at all but merely as a means of making one of the dialogical partners subservient to the other one. It becomes a form of discursive enslavement. And when that happens, then, truly, it is not only the enslaved person who is oppressed but the enslaver as well. For, a slaveholder has already diminished his own humanity because he has allowed himself to become something ethically vile and therefore existentially lesser. He has become a "colonist," an emotional and political cannibal, who, in diminishing and feeding off of those around him in order to hoard up power, has diminished himself by becoming, himself, a slave to his own greed, corruption, and darkness. The French Existentialist philosopher Albert Camus summed this up beautifully when he said, "The jailer is bound to the prisoner."

However, when instead of being seen as a dilemma, boundaries are affirmed as a positive occasion for discovery of self and other in an additive spirit, then they become the starting point for creative conversation between people on both sides of the boundary. The authors call this "additive boundary-crossing." Additive boundary crossing sparks a process of mutual enlightenment, providing members from both Culture A and B salutary opportunities to examine their own cultural practices in the light of other cultural practices.

Additive boundary-crossing may result in a member of Culture A: 1) reaffirming one of his cultural practices or perspectives in a more genuinely informed and courageously self-reflective manner; 2) modifying his cultural practice or perspective in light of his experience of Culture B's practices or perspectives, which, in this instance, he may find better than his own, at least in some respects; 3) synthesizing his cultural approach with that of Culture B; or 4) abandoning one of his cultural practices or perspectives and adopting that of Culture B since he has come to find B's approach better in some way. Of course, members of Culture B need to do the same things in their examination of and communication with Culture A.

When cultural differences are not seen, then, as *borders*, which (strictly defined and nervously guarded) cannot be crossed, but as more permeable boundaries that allow the free-flow of information, then *difference* becomes the foundation for constructive communication, not destructive domination. There are, as we will see later in this chapter, various ways to honor and cultivate the presence of subcultural borders in the classroom so that teachers and students will all be psychosocially and intellectually richer for the experience. Those who know how to promote such productive conversation between two or more cultures or subcultures are called *cultural negotiators.*

In the multicultural classroom, it is vital that teachers learn to act as cultural negotiators. There is no simple way or one book that can accomplish this for a teacher. [1] It requires experience of and respect for a wide variety of cultures—especially those that tend to be represented in one's classroom—a willingness to study other cultures both formally and informally, and the courage for the teacher to reflect upon his own culture and that of the classroom (and to accept the possibility of modifying both) in the light of his deepening experience of diversity. These are not easy things to do but the payoff is great for the teacher and his students.

Although different fields involving human services have varying definitions and practices regarding cultural competence, they tend to emphasize the following three criteria. A practitioner should: 1) gain an awareness of her own cultural assumptions, beliefs, and biases—what we have called cultural reflectivity; (2) cultivate knowledge of the worldviews of culturally different others; and (3) develop appropriate strategies and techniques for promoting intercultural awareness and cooperation in others (Sue et al., 1996).

CULTURE AND EDUCATION

Embedded both physically and symbolically within a society, schools reflect and reinforce a culture's patterns of interpersonal communication, ethical norms, social arrangements, historic and religious traditions, and definitions of what an "individual" is and what his roles and rights are. Thus, all of the issues discussed above come to bear in the classroom.

There are three ways in which a culture impresses upon the developing child what it means to be a student: how to relate to a teacher, to fellow students, and to the subjects being studied in the classroom.

These three things may vary considerably from culture to culture.

1. Any teaching and learning situation rests upon a foundation—sometimes only implied, sometimes made explicitly clear—about what kinds of goals and activities a culture values both inside and outside the classroom.
2. The culture provides the teacher and learner with tools and materials to meet the goals and support those values.

3. There exist "high-level cultural structures" (e.g., scripts, routines, and rituals) that are considered appropriate and useful in implementing the goals and values in socially harmonious ways. These three subsystems both assist and constrain the cognitive development of the child. They define for him the meaning of "teaching" and "learning," and they delineate what the "proper" roles of a teacher and student are. Moreover, they channel his thinking in ways appropriate to and supportive of his culture (Gauvain, 2001).

Culture-specific messages also shape the developing child along the following educationally significant lines. For, it is from his culture that a child: 1) learns "problem solving skills" (strategies to use and the knowledge-base to develop in order to recognize and approach and negotiate a problem); 2) develops "memory" (which entails absorbing cultural values in the form of memories of "exemplary situations" and learning specific strategies for remembering); and 3) learns the rules for "planning" (or learning how to coordinate one's own actions in order to reach goals as well as the rules for how to coordinate one's plans with those of others).

Where there is cultural congruity between a teacher's and student's worldview in these respects, there is a much greater chance that the child will succeed in his schooling. However, to the degree that such congruity between the student's culturally conditioned view of education does not fit with that of the teacher and the school, the chances of the student not succeeding in the classroom increase (Gauvain, 2001). This is not necessarily because the student is cognitively *deficient*. It is often simply because he is culturally *different*.

When a student has academic problems in a classroom because of this lack of "fit" between his culture's view of what education means and how it should be carried on, and the teacher's view of these things, then we say that the child's educational problems are a question of *cultural discontinuity* between his views and those of the teacher. Both the student's and teacher's understanding of educational settings and processes are possibly quite valid.

For instance, a student from an Asian culture may see the classroom as a place where students silently and respectfully record what the teacher says in order to memorize that knowledge and produce it on a test. On the other hand, the American teacher may feel that for education to be taking place, students must be actively and visibly engaged in asking questions and even from time to time challenging the teacher—something that would be highly inappropriate in Asian culture. Who is right? This teacher or this student?

Clearly, it is not a question of right and wrong. It is a question of equally valid but different approaches. However, it is almost always the teacher who holds the power in this situation. For the teacher to use his power in an enlightened way—which means being true to his vision of education and nurturing his student in it at the same time as he is sincerely honoring the student's worldview and meaningfully incorporating it into the shared culture of the classroom—this is the great challenge for the teacher in the multicultural educational settings of the twenty-first century.

These are pressing issues considering that most technologically advanced and economically prosperous nations in the world today are comprised of many different cultures and subcultures. What is more, those different cultures and subcultures have often historically had differential access to power and opportunity in those societies. Clearly, therefore, schools in a culturally pluralistic society, inevitably reflecting the norms and assumptions of the dominant culture, easily may—even with the best intentions—marginalize students who come from minority cultures. And intentions are not always the best.

Indeed, certain schools may even be engaged in a program of "educating" minority students *out of* the norms and assumptions of their cultures. This was certainly the case with Indian education in the United States. Native American students were often taken from their homes and tribes, sent across the country so that there was no possibility of escaping and returning to their families, forced to dress in European clothing, punished severely for using their own language, and rewarded only to the extent that they would "act white." As Adams has so poignantly put it, this was "education for extinction (Adams, 1995)."

Although the case of American Indian education was admittedly a dire one, U.S. schooling has promoted, and often enough enforced, the dominant culture's worldview on members of minority, or subdominant, groups. [2]

The multiculturally sensitive teacher strives to create a shared culture in the classroom, not impose one. This is even the case when the teacher is teaching the curriculum defined by the state, for that is usually the knowledge that provides students with socioeconomic power. It is the teacher's responsibility to make sure that his students have access to such knowledge—a point made a century ago by Harvard-educated African-American scholar W. E. B. Du Bois, and one that is still relevant today.

However, as the lead author has argued elsewhere, even where such "normative" knowledge is the curricular focus, the teacher should invite various cultural perspectives on it so that each student can view the curriculum with a critical eye, not simply slavishly accept it. He can appropriate from it what is psychosocially useful to him. He can also enrich his cultural worldview by appropriating the critiques of the curriculum by students from other cultures. In this way, he deepens his view of life, and his interactions with others grow more truly respectful.

By now it should be clear that schooling may wittingly or unwittingly serve *culturally conformist* goals. From a conservative point of view, this is the way it should be, for it is a conservative educational maxim that the predominant culture in a pluralistic society has the inherent right to "call all the shots" educationally. There is little or no room for other cultural ways of seeing, being, and doing things in the world in general and in the classroom specifically other than the ways that are favored by the dominant culture.

According to the conservative view, the task for a student from a minority culture is to learn how to *think* and *act* like a member of the dominant culture, even (indeed, especially) when that culture's norms run counter to those of his culture. Of course, this requires him to turn his back on his own culture, which often boils down to turning his back on his family, friends, and community in order to achieve educational and socioeconomic success.

In our view, this confronts the student with a lose-lose scenario: either lose his culture to gain socioeconomic success in the dominant culture, or relinquish educational and socioeconomic success in order to maintain his culture. To have to renounce one's culture in order to succeed educationally is education in the service of "deculturalization" (Spring, 2003). As a form of oppression by means of educational colonialism, it is neither ethically defensible nor pedagogically productive, for it inevitably does harm to a student.

According to a school of educational sociology known as "Resistance Theory," a great deal of subdominant student failure stems from that student's conscious or unconscious resistance to deculturalization, to playing the games necessary to be educationally successful when the price of success is denial of his own culture's norms and perspectives. Resistance is even more probable if the teacher or the school overtly disrespects the student's culture in some way. And even for the student who might be willing to pay the price of cultural self-denial in order to succeed, the pressure exerted by peers from his (sub)cultural group will often convince him to do otherwise (Wax, Wax, & Dumont, 1964).

Peer pressure is difficult to resist throughout the life span, but it is particularly difficult for a young person of school age, especially an adolescent, for whom peers are developmentally central in his evolving psychosocial sense of himself (Conger & Galambos, 1997).

Thus, when for whatever reasons a teacher is teaching in a way that runs counter to his students' cultural norms regarding what knowledge is, what knowledge is important, and how to interact with the teacher and his classmates in arriving at and using that knowledge, then the student is liable to either consciously or unconsciously resist "learning." For, the *cultural discontinuity* between the teacher's understanding of the processes and goals of education and that of the student are so different that this discontinuity disrupts the communication between the teacher and student and derails the educational endeavor.

All of this is not to say that the dominant culture's worldviews should be erased or demonized. In the authors' admittedly conservative opinion in this regard, this amounts to little more than reverse discrimination. It is simply to say that the various cultural perspectives represented in the classroom, including that of the dominant culture, should play a significant role in shaping the curriculum and the culture of the classroom.

Although cultural discontinuity may affect any aspect of education, language and literacy issues in the classroom provide a particularly dramatic example of the effects of cultural discontinuity in the classroom. This is because the interaction between literacy and cultural identity is so psychosocially complex and emotionally charged.

Literacy "in large part, involves facility in manipulating the symbols that codify and represent the values, beliefs, and norms of the culture—the same symbols that incorporate the culture's representations of reality" (Ferdman, 1990, p. 187). Since education from the earliest years to the highest academic levels involves becoming "literate" in various discursive contexts and curricular domains, it is therefore important for the teacher to know that

> literacy goes beyond superficial transaction with a printed or written page and extends into the ability to comprehend and manipulate its symbols—the words and concepts—and to do so in a culturally appropriate manner. . .So it is that literacy instruction can constitute a profound form of socialization. . .In the case of a majority child attending majority schools, this is essentially transparent in that neither educator nor pupil need consciously attend to the ways in which they are engaged in a process of cultural transmission. . .For members of cultural minorities, the potential conflicts will be greater, as will the salience of group membership. (Ferdman, 1990, p. 188–89)

Au and Kawakami have shown just how powerful cultural factors can be in literacy instruction. In a short but seminal article entitled "'Talk Story' and Learning to Read," they recount their experiences teaching reading to low-SES Hawaiian children.

Au and Kawakami wanted to devise culturally congruent ways of teaching standard content in the classroom because the typical means of instruction that had been used previously with these students—from well intentioned but culturally uninformed white teachers—had not worked. Casting off what they called "conventional school practices" in reading instruction, the authors decided instead to "talk story." "Talk story" is a crucial aspect of South Pacific Islander discourse and one that these children often bring with them to the classroom. "Talk story" is

> an important nonschool speech event for Hawaiian children. . . . During talk story, the children present rambling narratives about personal experiences, often joking and teasing one another. The chief characteristic of talk story is *joint performance*, or the cooperative production of responses by two or more speakers. . . . Thus, there are few times during talk story when just one child monopolizes the right to speak. . . . [W]hat is important to Hawaiian children in talk story is not *individual performance* in speaking, which is often impor-

tant in the [traditional] classroom, but *group performance* speaking. . . . [T]alk story-like reading lessons. . .are not exactly like nonschool talk story events. They are easily recognized as reading lessons in purpose, because discussion is focused closely on the text and text-related topics. In practice, then, talk story-like reading lessons are actually hybrid events, having the same goals for instruction as other classroom reading comprehension lessons, but making use of different rules for participation. (Au & Kawakami, 1985, pp. 407–10)

When Au and Kawakami allowed students to use "talk story" in learning how to read, their performance skyrocketed from its past abysmal showing to truly outstanding showings, individually and collectively. A culturally congruent pedagogy made all the difference. Again, the students were not deficient. They were different. By taking an additive view of this difference in the classroom, Au and Kawakami created a shared culture in the classroom in which all could succeed.

Of course, it is often not possible for a teacher to know all the subtleties, all the ins and outs, of teaching and learning in all of his students' cultures. However, the multiculturally wise teacher: 1) knows and honors the fact that such multiplicity exists; 2) is willing to discover more about it in the course of his teaching experiences and further studies; 3) learns how to draw in significant ways upon different cultural perspectives in determining what to study in the classroom and how to teach it; and 4) carries on the discourse of the classroom in a way that invites rich classroom discussions from various cultural points of view on the topics under analysis in the classroom. He thereby does himself and his students a great service—interpersonally, intellectually, and ethically—by making multiple cultural perspectives accessible in analyzing established ideas and creating new ones.

This requires that a teacher be—a *cultural negotiator* in his classroom. Although this can be a highly challenging role to fill, it is incumbent upon the twenty-first-century teacher to find ways in the classroom to help students from multiple (sub)cultures to understand their differences as *boundaries*, not *borders*. When the teacher takes and implements this additive view of cultural diversity in the classroom, it can magically transform that educational space from a battleground into a venue where students can arrive at ever deeper insights into themselves and others. In our view, this is the central purpose of education.

One way to make this happen is for the teacher and his students to become what Shirley Bryce Heath has called "ethnographic detectives." When students are ethnographic detectives, they *investigate* each other's cultures (Heath, 1983).

Virtually any activity or topic in a classroom can be an occasion for students from one culture to explore how that activity is to be done or how that topic is to be understood from the cultural vantage point of classmates from other cultures. The curriculum—even the most traditional one, which cannot be ignored if only because it is the knowledge that buys students socioeconomically empowering skills and knowledge in society—may thus become an occasion for each student to investigate his fellow classmates' different worldviews.

Under the guidance of a culturally sensitive teacher, exploration of various cultures can encourage students to stop taking their own cultural norms (whether dominant or subdominant) as simply "given" and unquestionably "true," even "superior," and begin to look at their culture more analytically and sometimes even critically. A student thereby learns to *examine*, not merely *enact*, his own culture's points-of-view and practices.

This process of *cultural reflectivity*, is, as we suggested earlier in this chapter, key to a humane and inclusive sensibility in the contemporary world, and it is also key to a student's personal maturation emotionally and ethically (Spindler & Spindler, 1987). These must be primary educational *desiderata* in today's world.

A final way to create multiculturally healthy classrooms is to help students from subdominant cultures engage in "cool alternation." *Cool alternation* occurs when a person takes on new cultural roles in a given situation but does so in small increments, self-reflectively, and with open and frequent discussions among all the participants engaged in the process. In this way, no one is pushed too far or too fast out of their cultural comfort zones. This promotes the psychosocially healthy process of mutual "accommodation" without forcing upon students the psychosocially damaging process of "assimilation," wherein everyone must learn to dance to the tune of the dominant culture (Gibson, 1988).

Cool alternation allows various cultural perspectives to weave in and out of each other so as to create a tapestry of truly democratic empowerment for one and all. Cool alternation offers ways of forging a common classroom culture out of many perspectives, thus embodying educationally the great political principle: *E pluribus unum*.

Cool alternation is an example of what sociologists call "secondary socialization"—which means learning about one's new roles in new cultural contexts. Cool alternation accomplishes this without deculturalization, which, as we have seen, entails the painful process of being forced to renounce one's own culture and its roles in order to unquestioningly, totally, and immediately fit into a new culture—in other words, educational colonialism. Cool alternation is the best way to help students adapt to a new classroom culture, for it allows them to learn the "cultural vocabulary" of the new school without negating their natal culture.

When students from subdominant cultures are allowed to decide for themselves what parts of the dominant culture they may wish to accept for their own purposes so that they do not have to commit cultural suicide in order to do well in school, they will—as predicted by Resistance Theory—be much less likely to resist school and fail in it as a means of maintaining their cultural identity and integrity. They can "coolly" alternate between their own culture and the dominant culture at will, becoming more empowered in the process.

Again, however, it must be stressed that teachers, already overtaxed with a wide variety of onerous mandates as well as unfair public misperceptions about their difficult work, cannot be expected to do and know everything. However, simply being aware of these cultural issues, having some familiarity with the tools and techniques that have been discussed, and—above all—simply and truly caring about all of their students go a very long way in fostering a constructive, additive multicultural atmosphere in the classroom.

Holistic Multicultural Education

In the lead author's book, *Understanding the Whole Student: Holistic Multicultural Education,* Clifford examines in-depth multicultural education across the range of holistic domains: the organic, psychodynamic, affiliative, procedural, and existential (2007). It is beyond the scope of this book to present all of that information here. In this section, then, we will mention just a few of the most salient multicultural educational issues in the organic and psychodynamic domains—the two areas that we have dealt with in the two previous chapters.

CULTURE AND EDUCATION IN THE ORGANIC DOMAIN

At the sensory-motor domain, perhaps the first thing to notice is that a great deal of what happens in the typical classroom is carried on verbally, not at the sensory-motor level—and more and more so with each higher grade. This is not true of all cultures, however. Hence, the extreme emphasis on language in the normative American classroom can create educational problems for students where language is used less frequently, or used differently, than in the standard American classroom.

In Native American culture, for instance, a child learns many of his most important lessons nonverbally from parents and elders, largely through eye contact, body language, and even silence as a sign of approval or disapproval of the child's performance on a certain task. Entering a typical public school, therefore, a Native American student often experiences obstacles because, based on his culture's views of teaching and learning, he comes to the classroom "expecting freedom of movement, but discover[s] restrictive movement; where visual spatial kinesthetic learning was the mode, the verbal dimension is stressed; where direct experience had been the route for learning, now most experience is indirect. . ." (Pepper, 1989, p. 37).

Native American modes of teaching and learning styles are visual largely because there is a premium placed on observing how elders do things and then observing the elders' body language and facial gestures regarding one's performance. In general, indeed, Native American culture puts much greater stock in actual performance than in mere talk. It is not surprising, therefore, that "Native children are able to efficiently and effectively process and retain information presented through visual formats" and less through classroom talk (Kaulback, 1989, p. 141).

Especially from the middle-school years on, however, a great deal of teaching in standard classrooms consists of unbroken streams of teacher-talk, with little chance for the student to learn through observation or to demonstrate mastery through performance. When this is the case, the cultural discontinuity between the Native American's preferred sensory modes of learning, on one hand, and the talk that dominates the typical classroom, on the other hand, may be so great that the Native American student may feel disoriented, excluded, or threatened.

The result is this student failing academically, which may easily be misinterpreted as stemming from cognitive deficiency or a bad attitude in the student whereas, in fact, the problem may well be the radical discontinuity between his culture's understanding of the process of education and that which governs the culture of the classroom.

But in a classroom where at least some of the teaching and learning are conducted in kinesthetic and visual modes, then the Native American student, able to "hold onto" something and more likely to feel included in what is going on in the classroom, is more apt to build upon those positive feelings and to succeed. What is more, other students—whose personal or cultural preferences may not be visual or kinesthetic—can benefit by learning to operate in nonverbal ways, too.

And this highlights one of the great advantages of holistic education—namely, that when education is carried on holistically, the preferred styles of all cultural groups are honored, and members from a particular group—whether they come from a dominant or subdominant culture—can grow by being more broadly and systematically exposed to other group's ways of approaching tasks and creating knowledge.

Another example of differential sensory-motor preferences comes from Barbara Shade, one of the most prominent researchers of preferred learning styles among African-American students.

Shade speaks of "the kinesthetic preference" of many African-American K-12 students. She notes that African-American childrearing practices tend to be more physically dynamic than those in many White families. Hence, it is sometimes true that an African-American student will tend to respond best in the classroom to "spontaneity and ability for improvisation and rhythmic orientation which is shown in body movements, music, art forms, verbal and nonverbal communication patterns, and other artistic expressions" (Shade, 1989, p. 26).

It is very important to bear in mind that these are generalities and should be applied with caution to any individual student. Not all African-American students fit the above descriptions by Shade about "typical" African-American learning styles any more than a member of any other culture necessarily conforms to his culture's "typical" styles. But when used cautiously and sensitively, such typifications may prove valuable in helping a teacher carry on the business of the classroom in a way that addresses, to the greatest degree that is practicable, the culturally based educational styles of all of his students.

Another consideration at the organic level is the fact that an increasing number of students in the public school classrooms have experienced a wide range of emotional, socioeconomic, and political traumas in their lives that have had physical consequences for the students (Bullough, 2001).

Such trauma, ranging from witnessing war, to having been targeted in programs of ethnic cleansing, to gang violence, and having being sexually abused "leaves its traces not just in people's minds but in their muscles and skeletons as well" (Fay, 1987, p. 146). Indeed, the trauma may first imprint itself on a child at an organic level before it crystallizes into a conscious thought. "Somatic patterns are part of the experiences which eventually become internalized at a representational level" (Greenspan, 1989, p. 234). More and more teachers are seeing these physical signs of trauma in their students.

These psychological and political traumas engrave themselves on the body of the child as a wide range of physical symptoms such as facial and bodily tics; hyperactivity; panic attacks; physical clinging to adults and exorbitant neediness, on one hand, or physical and emotional detachment from and unresponsiveness to adults, on the other hand; sexual promiscuity and perversion; physically aggressive behavior against classmates; overly suggestive clothing sexually; and riddling the body with garish and excessive piercings and tattoos.

Added to this is the damage done by current cultural standards in our culture regarding physical attractiveness in females. Little girls learn from an early age that they are seen as sexual objects and that in order to be desirable they must conform to an image of femininity that is really nothing more than male corporate executives' adolescent fantasies of what a woman should look like and be. To get the "right" look, an increasing number of girls will torture their bodies into stylish proportions, developing eating disorders or taking amphetamine-type drugs to lose weight.

Among boys, eating disorders are less common although still significant. However, it is not unusual for boys to risk their lives with steroids so that they can conform to the image and attain the performance levels of their favorite athletic culture-heroes—men whose unhealthy conquests, both on and off the field, create a pathological model of masculinity for boys across the ethnic and socioeconomic spectrum in the United States today.

The Classroom as Physically Therapeutic

What can teachers—who are neither physicians nor therapists—do to address, in some measure at least, these culturally conditioned organic pathologies that are showing up in increasing numbers of students?

What they can do is simple but enormously healthful. They can offer the student a physically rich learning environment that recognizes and nurtures him or her as a multi-sensory, culturally embedded being. Just having such a place to come to each day can be immensely restorative to young people. Such physically robust and culturally respectful spaces benefit all students, not just those who have suffered particularly high degrees of trauma. Indeed, the physically healthy classroom provides

> a connectedness with the world of nature and the physical universe; physical health, a love and appreciation for the body and good maintenance; good capacity for expression through the body, through voice, gesture, and facial movements; the development of physical skills and the capacity to do things well with the hands; a greater capacity for enjoyment and enhanced sensory awareness, thus eliminating boredom; good respect and care for objects; a positive self-image with the confidence that accompanies it; a capacity to liberate energy that is encapsulated in the body through past emotional traumas and experiences, so that psychological problems are not retained in the body. . .(Whitmore, 1986, pp. 42).

CULTURE AND EDUCATION IN THE PSYCHODYNAMIC DOMAIN

In chapter 2 we saw how inextricably bound emotions and cognition are. Education is a complex emotional experience. And what is more, emotions are largely a *cultural* phenomenon. Emotions do not arise or develop in a social vacuum. To the contrary! They arise and develop in the culture(s) in which a person lives, moves, and has his being. Hence, because emotions are so culturally saturated and so educationally important, let us look briefly at some of the major aspects of the interplay between culture and emotions.

These are important things for the teacher to know. The emotions that a student evidences in the classroom—which may emerge with an almost electric force and speed in how he responds (either positively or negatively) to the teacher, the curriculum, and his classmates—are often inseparable from the student's cultural identity.

Emotion, Culture, and the Self

The emotional "sculpting" of the child by his culture(s) is accomplished in three interrelated ways, according to the social psychologist John Hewitt (Hewitt, 1984, pp.161-162).

First, our emotions "arise naturally in our efforts to complete individual and social acts." This means simply that when we are doing something, either alone or with others, the action is usually accompanied by some type and degree of emotion. The things we do, think, and feel are interrelated.

Second, says Hewitt, our emotions are "an experience of self." *We know who we are by how we feel* about things and situations, yet how we feel about things and situations is often a matter of how our culture has taught us we *should* feel. In this manner, a person's "experience" of his "self"—his sense of "identity" and his degree of "self esteem," which are crucial educationally—is an emotional fact that is affected by his culture's norms.

In other words, a person finds a major portion of his identity by how well he "fits in with" others in the culture and subcultures with which he identifies—his *reference groups*, so called because he defines and evaluates himself in reference to their standards. According to the psychiatrist Alfred Adler (1930), this "social feeling" is a prime motivator of our behavior.

We spend a good deal of our day involved in what Goffman has termed "impression management" and "face work"—those dialogues with others as well as our internal talk with a introjected "Generalized Other" through which we assure ourselves and others that we "get the rules," are "living by them," and are "good" people (Goffman, 1997, p. 109). Impression management and face work are key in the efficient operation of any culture. Problems can arise, however, if a person finds that one of his cultural beliefs or practices is morally unacceptable or psychologically painful in some other context that is also important to him.

And this is precisely what is happening when he is experiencing high degrees of cultural discontinuity in the classroom. Then he must face the agonizing decision of whether to *conform* to his native but now problematic cultural norm (by which he has defined himself) or *resist* it, even *reject* it, and thereby risk being ostracized from his culture (and losing a sense of his identity) in order to gain acceptance into the new group. Violating one's cultural norms is no small step to take and it often exacts a heavy emotional toll. *Not* meeting one's cultural standards and expectations often breeds anxiety and depression.

Third, Hewitt points out that our emotions "are a regular part of the role-making process" (1984, p. 70). An individual's sense of identity and feelings of self-esteem largely grow out of *what roles* he plays in his culture and *how well* he feels that he plays them. A role is "a place to stand as one participates in social acts. It provides the perspective from which one acts. . . ." What is more, "the roles of others, through our own acts of imagination, provide perspectives from which we view both their conduct and our own."

Our emotion-laden evaluations of ourselves and others reflects how we: 1) *judge others* on the basis of how well *we* feel they are playing *their* roles and 2) *judge ourselves* on the basis of how we feel that *they* feel we are playing *our* roles (Hewitt, 1984, p. 61).

Each of these roles entails: 1) certain emotions to be felt and expressed at different levels of intensity and openness depending upon the situation; 2) various types of body language and degrees of physical closeness; 3) certain words, expressions and even grammatical forms that one will use depending upon the person with whom one is talking; and even 4) different visions of one's place and purpose in the universe.

Multicultural students are often required to play so many different roles during the day, in the classroom and outside of it, that it might well boggle the mind of a person from a dominant culture to even consider them. Not only is this a cognitively and socially complex set of tasks. It is an emotionally high-stakes endeavor—especially when one feels that one is failing in a role that he wishes to succeed in but can make little sense out of culturally, or when a role is being forced upon him that violates his culturally rooted sense of who he is.

To the extent that a teacher can help a student negotiate these difficult cultural dances, he proves a true friend and an adept cultural negotiator to the student who in so many ways looks to the teacher for help and guidance in a classroom that may be a culturally problematic, even perilous, zone for him.

An Overview of Research and Practice in Second-Language Acquisition

Language is a preeminent tool, and perhaps *the* preeminent tool, in the forming and maintenance of a culture. Since the acquisition of English as a second language is such a vital educational issue at every educational level from kindergarten to graduate school in the United States today, we now present an overview of some of the most important research, theories and practices regarding the acquisition of a second language (L2).

We provide this overview so that the classroom teacher, armed with this basic knowledge from the field of applied linguistics, may be more sensitive to the language issues that many of his students are facing as they are simultaneously attempting to come to grips with a new language, culture, and set of educational practices.

Three of the most important researchers in L2 acquisition today are Stephen Krashen (2003), Jim Cummins (1997), and Virginia Collier (1995).

KRASHEN'S FIVE HYPOTHESES ABOUT L2 ACQUISITION

Stephen Krashen's five hypotheses about how a second language is acquired have been highly influential in the training of ESL teachers for decades and are useful for all teachers to know.

Krashen's first hypothesis regards what he calls the Acquisition-Learning Distinction. He claims that language *acquisition* is a subconscious process while language *learning* is a conscious one. Students acquiring a language are usually unaware that they are doing so; rather, they are simply aware that they are using the L2 for communication. On the other hand, learning a language involves knowing grammatical rules and being able to talk about them. Students *acquire* an L2 in just "carrying on" in the classroom and on the playground, not to mention in the outside world, from day to day. This is just as important as *learning* the L2 through explicit language instruction.

Second is the Natural Order Hypothesis. Simply stated, this "hypothesis claims that grammatical structures are acquired (not learned) in a predictable order. Certain structures tend to 'come' early, others later" (Krashen, 1981, p. 51).

Krashen's third hypothesis is the Monitor Hypothesis. This is perhaps the best known of the five hypotheses. It adds more information about the acquisition-learning distinction by pointing out that in most cases

> acquisition "initiates" our utterances in a second language and is responsible for our fluency. Learning has only one function, and that is as a monitor or editor. Learning comes into play only to make changes in the form of our utterance, after it has been "produced" by the acquired system. (Krashen, 1982, p. 15)

The "monitor" can become a problem if a student is so overly concerned about the correctness of every utterance that he ties himself up in knots of linguistic self-vigilance! It is important for a teacher to bear in mind that, although the goal is for the student to become near-natively fluent, this will happen most smoothly and quickly if the teacher does not overcorrect the student to such an extent that the student begins to overcorrect himself because of an overactive monitor. Learning a language requires taking risks and making mistakes—sometimes rather embarrassing ones—in a variety of speech-situations and social contexts.

If a student is always monitoring himself perfectionistically, he will not take those risks. Consequently, he will become fluent, if at all, in a much slower and more painful way than if he did take risks. Ironically, in L2 learning, the desire to speak perfectly can be the greatest obstacle to progress. The overcorrecting teacher can impede L2 acquisition. This is important for the teacher to remember.

Krashen maintains that his fourth hypothesis, the Comprehensible Input Hypothesis, is the most important of all five because it answers the question of how language is acquired. How does an individual move from understanding something in L2 at level X to understanding something at the next level of competence in the L2, level X+1? The answer is that he must be able to comprehend most of the input that is contained in utterance X. The rest of the utterance—that is, the new +1 part of the utterance—can be understood and then learned by the student by his piecing together various kinds of contextual clues from X that reveal the +1 meaning.

In other words, if the learner understands most of what is being said in an utterance—if the input is comprehensible—then he can generally draw fairly accurate inferences about the part of the utterance that he does not understand from the context provided by what he does understand. Says Krashen, "we use more than our linguistic competence to help us understand. We also use context, our knowledge of the world, our extra-linguistic information to help us understand language directed at us" (Krashen, 1982, p. 21).

We infer from context, in other words, and this is how L2 students often "pick up" words, expressions, and grammatical forms without explicit instruction about them. The important lesson for the teacher here is that he try to offer the L2 student material and engage him in tasks that go just a little beyond what he already knows but that provide sufficient context for the student to be able to *naturally* infer meanings and definitions.

The Affective Filter Hypothesis is Krashen's final hypothesis. This hypothesis explains how emotional factors such as motivation, self-confidence, and anxiety affect the process of L2 acquisition—all issues that we discussed in the previous chapter regarding the psychodynamics of education. If the teacher, classmates, the school as an institution, and the society at large take a positive view of students who are attempting to learn English as a second language, those students—sensing that nurturance—will learn English more quickly and in a more positive frame of mind than if they are meeting with suspicion, criticism, and fear.

Learning a second language in a new culture is a highly emotional process—as anyone who has ever had that experience can attest to—and it requires emotional support. As teachers, we need to be in the front line of offering that support and helping the community understand why it should also support our "Limited English Proficiency" (LEP) students.

CUMMINS'S BASIC INTERPERSONAL COMMUNICATION
SKILLS (BICS), COGNITIVE ACADEMIC LANGUAGE
PROFICIENCY SKILLS (CALPS), AND COMMON UNDERLYING
PROFICIENCY (CUP)

According to Jim Cummins, there are three types of L2 proficiency. First is conversational fluency. Cummins uses the phrase Basic Interpersonal Communication Skills (BICS) to describe this phenomenon. It takes approximately one to two years for a student to develop BICS. Second is discrete language skills. These "reflect specific phonological, literacy, and grammatical knowledge that students acquire as a result of direct instruction and both formal and informal practice (e.g., reading)" (Cummins, 2000, p. 64). Discrete skills develop early, at the same time that BICS are developing. Third is Cognitive Academic Language Proficiency Skills (CALPS), which refers to the form of L2 that a student must master in order to succeed in the classroom. While BICS are acquired within one to two years, CALPS require anywhere from four to seven years to develop. The difference between BICS and CALPS consists in the fact that

> when English language learners reach a stage in their schooling (from fourth grade upward) where cognitive and academic language skills become of paramount importance, they hit a wall of complexity [that is, the CALPS level] that their basic conversational skills cannot penetrate, and at that point they fall further and further behind . . . unless specific steps are taken to develop their academic-linguistic competence. (Cummins, 2000, p. 202).

A final component of Cummins theory is the Transfer Hypothesis, which is that prior knowledge and skills in the home language (L1) transfer to the new language. This is so, Cummins argues, because if a student learns how to perform a task in his native L1, he can transfer those skills to solving a similar task in his new L2. A student who has learned to set up, carry out, and then report on a chemistry experiment in Spanish will be able to use that same set of conceptual skills to perform another experiment using English. His chemistry experiments in Spanish and English rely on a Common Underlying Proficiency (CUP).

The point here—and one that is crucial in the argument for bilingual education—is that what is learned in a student's L1 is not lost in the process of the student learning an L2. Indeed, a student learns an L2 all the more quickly and correctly if his L2 instruction builds upon—and does not neglect or negate—his L1 experiences, proficiencies, and psychosocial attachments. This argument is eminently sensible in the light of findings in cognitive psychology that students learn new concepts and skills by building upon ones that they have already mastered (Solso, 1998).

COLLIER'S L1-MAINTENANCE/L2-DEVELOPMENT PEDAGOGY

Virginia Collier's work is in many respects a synthesis and extension of Krashen's and Cummins's work.

Like Krashen, Collier believes that there is an "affective filter," which is a combination of social and emotional factors, that is central to how, and how well, a student will learn. If a student feels emotionally and socially validated by his teacher, classmates, and institution, he is much more likely to be successful in his academic performance and general social involvement in the school.

These psychosocial factors "may include individual student variables such as self-esteem or anxiety or other affective factors" (Collier, 1995, p. 2). If a student feels emotional warmth and cultural respect from his teacher and peers, he has a much better chance of succeeding in the classroom than if he does not.

Like Cummins, Collier feels that what a student learns in his L1 will transfer into his L2—not only with no loss but with considerable gain since: 1) the student is learning to be competent in two different languages; and 2) the skills that the student possesses in his L1 can enrich his performance in his L2 in various ways, just as the skills he learns in the course of his mastery of his L2 can enrich his understanding of and performance in his L1. It is common, for instance, for someone to say, "I never really understood the grammar of my own language until I learned the grammar of a foreign language!" This is an example of L2 proficiency heightening L1 sensitivity and enhancing L1 use in a native L1 speaker.

Collier points out that as a student's grade level increases, so, of course, do the "vocabulary, sociolinguistic, and discourse dimensions of language" which that student must now confront (Collier, 1995, p. 3).

Collier is here alluding to Cummins's BICS/CALPS dichotomy. The problem, she goes on to point out, is that the rapidly increasing cognitive and linguistic demands on a student as he moves from grade to grade may be faster than his L2 development. When that happens—and it very often does, even for the best of L2 learners—then the nonnative English-speaking student, despite his most valiant efforts, will fall behind the other students in his academic development, which will, in turn, have a depressing effect on his L2 acquisition.

Thus, Collier argues for what are called "maintenance bilingual education programs"—so called because they maintain the student's L1 and continue to provide much, if not most and sometimes even all, of his classroom instruction in the L1, while helping him with his L2 development at other times in the school day.

It is essential that we provide non-native-English-speaking students with such programs, Collier claims, because if a student is trying to learn English at the same time as he is learning academic content in English, he must inevitably fall behind his peers, which will begin a downward spiral of decreasing academic success that will end catastrophically in general academic failure.

Maintenance Bilingual Education

The case for maintenance bilingual education is a strong one. In fact, many, if not most, of the people in the world are at least somewhat bilingual (Nieto, 2002, p. 90). In Switzerland, for instance, there are four official languages of the nation: German, French, Italian, and Romansh. In Canada, 10 percent of married couples are mixed-lingual. In the United States, about 32 million people (over 10 percent of the population) speak another language at home: 17 million speak Spanish, 2 million speak French, and a combined 1 million speak German, Italian, and Chinese.

We need to take an additive view of bilingualism in society and the schools, not a subtractive one, as is often the case today, especially in conservative political circles. According to the additive view, bilingualism, involving no loss of L1 while developing mastery of L2, generates many benefits, including: 1) higher cognitive development for the student; 2) greater and more varied linguistic resources within the school and society; and 3) increased cultural interaction and understanding, leading to the mutual enrichment of the cultures involved.

Lambert, another important L2 researcher, has demonstrated how people who are bilinguals have various cognitive advantages over monolinguals, including: 1) more expertise in their own L1; 2) better selective attention to subtle aspects of language; 3) more awareness of the arbitrariness of names of items; 4) more sensitivity to non-verbal elements of communication; 5) better ability at following complicated instructions; and 6) enhanced performance on tests of creativity, concept formation, and spatial ability (in Grossman, 1995).

One disadvantage that Lambert noted was that bilinguals are sometimes slightly slower than monolinguals in language processing speed—an important thing for teachers to keep in mind with administering timed tests to bilingual students, who may need a bit more time to complete the task. In general, however, research on bilingualism has shown it to represent an enormous "academic plus" if the bilingual program is a good and sustained one.

INTERLANGUAGE

As a person acquires a second language, he will speak and write different versions of the language as he advances from Stage A (at the beginning) to

Stages X, Y, and Z (as he attains high levels of proficiency that increasingly resemble the way native speakers speak L2). These versions are call interlanguages. An L2-interlanguage is not the same thing as the L2 itself, of course—although as the student becomes increasingly proficient in L2, his interlanguage comes more and more to resemble the native L2 usage.

However, it would not be accurate to dismiss interlanguages as merely "incorrect" versions of L2, as teachers sometimes understandably but incorrectly do. For, what second-language-acquisition researchers and teachers have found is that interlanguages tend to have their own internally consistent systems of pronunciation, vocabulary, and grammar, which the speakers of those interlanguages robustly employ with each other. Interlanguages are "composed of numerous elements [in which] the learners themselves impose structure on the available linguistic data and formulate an internalized system" (Gass & Selinker, 1994, p. 11).

Although students who are roughly at Stage E, say, of learning English do not speak English in a fully fluent way yet as they will at Stage Y (when they will have near-native proficiency), they are nevertheless speaking a rule-governed "language"—a internally consistent version of English that is "on the road" to becoming the L2. As such, speakers of L2/Stage-E, will often be able to communicate among themselves quite effectively in ways that their L2 teacher may not be able to totally understand.

CULTURE IN THE CLASSROOM—AND THE CULTURE OF THE CLASSROOM

In this chapter, we have looked at the pivotal role of culture in determining how smoothly and fruitfully, or how painfully and contentiously, the processes of education may unfold. Every teacher and student comes to the classroom with his or her own complex cultural makeup. They then find themselves in a classroom that is itself embedded in, and that therefore embodies, the norms of a dominant culture that generally expects those norms to be promoted in that classroom.

In a radically multicultural society such as the United States, however, it is not pedagogically wise, politically practicable, or ethically defensible to shove a dominant culture's worldview down the throats of students (and sometimes teachers, too) who come from subdominant cultures, and who are equally members of the society and have just as much to offer as does the dominant culture.

Unless education is to become largely a political program of forcing one set of cultural views and practices on various other cultural groups with somewhat different views and practices but who do not happen to be as politically powerful as the dominant culture, then we must acknowledge that cultural diversity is a positive, not a negative.

We must take the additive view that, at both the individual and collective levels, we all stand to benefit greatly from various cultural perspectives that allow us to use divergent points of view as ways of critiquing and creating knowledge, engendering and expanding vision, and sparking dynamic discourses that allow the the melding of various cultural worldviews without violating the essential integrity of any.

In short, whether one favors the "melting pot" or the "salad bowl" vision of the enlightened and energetic multicultural society, it behooves everyone involved in education to teach and learn in ways that are culturally sensitive, psychosocially healthy, cognitively dynamic, and, therefore, good for all.

APPLICATION: THE MULTI-CULTURE DIMENSION

Curriculum from the content areas provides a wonderful medium through which students can understand that while humanity is different in many ways, we have much in common in terms of our aspirations, values, and dreams. Teachers can design learning experiences from the heart of the core curriculum that cause students to develop respect for the richness of diversity within and across cultures, including multiple perspectives and respecting their own and others' life journeys.

MULTIPLE PERSPECTIVES

Students can develop the ability and disposition to see life's events from multiple perspectives through their studies in all content areas at all levels of K12 education. A few examples from literacy, science, and history follow.

Literature. Literature provides students with opportunities to examine human life from the perspectives of diverse individuals. Viewing humanity from different perspectives helps students to better find the truth of things, broaden their world view, and develop empathy for others. Through these processes, students can develop the capacity to see that humanity has more in common than first appears and to be comfortable with the differences. By gaining these understandings students can develop more self awareness and be better prepared to navigate life in the company of diverse individuals. Hopefully, students will realize that diversity is the norm of life, not the exception to which they must adjust. Following are some learning examples:

Through the ages, children have enjoyed the story of the "Three Little Pigs," the oldest version of which is narrated from the perspective of the three pigs. To the delight of readers, in recent years, this story has been told from many perspectives. One perspective, "The True Story of the Three

Little Pigs" by Jon Sciezka (1989), is told from the wolf's perspective in which he claims that he was completely innocent of the charges that put him in jail. From his perspective, he was just coming to the house of the three pigs to borrow a cup of sugar and the crimes he was charged with were all in their imagination. Another version of that story, "The Fourth Little Pig" by Teresa Celsi (1990), is told from the perspective of the sister of the three little pigs who was an adventurer. In this version she tells the pigs to quit cowering in their brick home and get out and live life. By reading and discussing all these versions, young students (and maybe even older ones) can develop their academic literacy skills while also becoming sensitive to the fact that actors in every life situation view it from their own unique lens.

A study of these versions of the original story "The Three Little Pigs" could yield many opportunities for students to appreciate the importance of being able to take multiple perspectives. Following are a sample of learning experiences teachers could use:

1. Discovering the facts. One of the most important things well-informed individuals do is to discover the truth of things; to do so requires individuals to look at all sides of issues. For instance, let us look at the situation of the three pigs. Individuals can get a much broader and more accurate understanding of the situation if they consider the situation from the perspective of all the actors, such as that of the big bad wolf. Teachers could have students complete a Venn diagram (figure 3.1) to compare and contrast the perspectives represented in the first version of the three pigs with the perspectives presented in the other two.

Content Areas. While the above versions of the Three Little Pigs may seem appropriate for young children only, they can provide a fun-loving entry point to the study of multiple perspectives for older students. Once teachers read multiples version of the Three Little Pigs, students can apply the study of multiple perspectives through other content areas, such as history.

Teachers could engage students in an in-depth study of important pivotal events in history, such as the *Brown v. Board of Education*, in U.S. history. After years of work, Thurgood Marshall and his team of lawyers from the

 Original Story of the Three Pigs

The Fourth Little Pig   The True Story of the Three Pigs

Figure 3.1

NAACP were successful in getting the 1896 *Plessy v. Ferguson* Supreme Court decision of "separate but equal" rendered unconstitutional. Through this decision, the U.S. States Supreme Court declared that segregated schooling was unconstitutional. Due to the controversial nature of the events leading to this decision and the cascade of events that followed, people held very different perspectives.

Students could examine all perspectives of this important event through preparing for and holding a debate. Students could prepare for this debate by first studying the core issues of how "separate but equal" played out in the public school system before and after the decision and then researching particular perspectives of the main players. Teachers could use a combination of the activities below to help students examine this issue from varied points of view.

1. Brainstorm the groups of actors involved in this issue and identify what their perspectives would likely be.
2. Divide the class into research teams, each of which will do an in-depth study of one set of actors and the unique perspective they held.
3. Use a jigsaw puzzle discussion in which students teach one another what they learned about the particular perspective they researched.
4. Hold a debate on the issue or a town meeting in which students speak from the unique perspective they researched.
5. Contrast the debate with a conversation for understanding by placing students in groups so that each group is made up of representatives from each perspective.
6. Culminate this study by having students write an in depth article on the *Brown v. Board of Education*, taking a historical perspective that represented the major views.

LEARNING FROM ONE'S LIFE JOURNEY

Each of us comes from somewhere. We carry our past—elements of our culture, a particular view of the world, and our hopes—into the future. In many ways our journeys are unique, but they also share many commonalities with the journeys of others. By helping students value their own life's journey, teachers also position themselves to appreciate the journey of others. This appreciation can be developed with students of all ages, even those who may not be in formal schooling. Following are some experiences that teachers could use to help students value their life journey while also developing an appreciation of the life journey of others.

Literature–Primary and Intermediate Grade Students. Reading stories and biographies about the journeys of fictional characters and real people helps students appreciate the life story of others. For example, they could read Patricia Polacco, a celebrated author of more than thirty-three children's books, most of which are autobiographical. Teachers could introduce the notion of life's journeys by sharing *The Keeping Quilt* (1998a), a story of the transformation of a quilt that Patricia's family made from their clothing in which Polacco recounts the peace this quilt brought as its use changed with each stage of Patricia's life.

Another story by Polacco is *Thank You, Mr. Falker* (1998c), a beautiful and true story of a fifth grade teacher who went to great lengths to teach Patricia, who suffered with dyslexia, to read. Another book, *My Rotten Red-headed Older Brother* (1998b), recounts her first awareness of how much her older brother loved her. From sharing these and other autobiographical stories by Polacco, teachers could have students do the following:

1. Compare and contrast Patricia Polacco's life journey with their own. Toward that end each student could design two keeping quilts, one for Polacco and one for their own life journey. Each quilt could be made up of pictures and symbols that represent important events in their lives. Once the quilts are designed students could compare and contrast the similarities and differences in Polacco's and their own lives.
2. Identify important transitions in Polacco's and their own lives, such as learning an important skill like reading or riding a bike, or gaining a new insight as Polacco did in the book, *My Rotten Red-headed Older Brother* (1998b). After examining Polacco's writing style, students could select one of their important transition events and produce their own picture book.

Language Arts for Intermediate and Secondary School Students. Older students could embark on examining their own life's journey through the study of Greek Mythology, adolescent literature, and/or the way people from various cultures represent their life stories.

For example this study could be kicked off by introducing students to Janus, a Roman God with two heads, who was blessed to see the past while simultaneously looking toward the future. To the Romans, he symbolized change and transitions, such as the progression of the past to the future, the shift from one condition to another, passage of one important life phase to another, of one vision to another, and of one universe to another. After being introduced to Janus, students could reflect on the insights they gleaned from their past and use them to forge a hopeful and successful future, through any of the following activities below:

1. The Newberry-winning book *Hatchet* by Gary Paulsen (2007) provides a study of a significant transformation made at a critical time by Brian Robeson who was angry at his parents' pending divorce. While flying in a small plane to visit his father, the pilot had a heart attack, which forced Brian to land the plane in a lake that was located in an isolated wilderness. His struggle to survive forced Brian to mature into a young man who was able to deal constructively with life's challenges. Students could write a reflective paper on an event in their lives in which they made an important transition in their thinking, abilities, or levels of maturity. This paper would be comprised of three sections:

   a. description of the event
   b. articulation of what they learned from the event
   c. explanation of how they will use what they learned for the future

2. Students could write of this transformational event in their lives using an autobiographical or fictional genre.

3. Students could learn various ways to depict their life stories by studying the story telling traditions of culturally diverse people. For example, a young Navajo artist in Canyon de Chelly depicted his life journey on a piece of slate using a spiral, with his infancy and childhood starting at the tightest point. The artist put a symbol to represent events and people that had influenced him on his life's journey as illustrated below. Students could make a story spiral that depicts their lives, placing symbols that represent their past within the spiral and those they desire or project for the future, on loosest end.

NOTES

1. However, the lead author's book *Understanding the Whole Student: Holistic Multicultural Education* (2007) offers a wide range of theories and pedagogical practices that can help the teacher become a more adept cultural negotiator in the classroom.

2. The use of the phrase "subdominant groups" is preferable to "minority groups" since a group may not be in the minority but may still have lesser chances in a society. This was the case, for instance, in the former Rhodesia, where blacks made up over 90 percent of the population but were still oppressed by the numerically lesser but politically hegemonic whites. Although the numerical majority, blacks were still politically subdominant—indeed, dominated.

Chapter Four

The Procedural Dimension

We are beings who inquire systematically into our world, and we do so largely through the various academic disciplines. These disciplines—each one steeped in its own procedures and terminology—correspond to, and to some extent give birth to, the different aspects of our intellectual experiences.

Physics, biology, chemistry, geology, astronomy, and all the other sciences and hybrid sciences have their special languages to go about their business. At the core of those languages is the universal scientific language: mathematics. That is why Immanuel Kant (1997), in his *Critique of Pure Reason*, called this kind of scientific knowing, with its various procedural systems, "mathetic."

The arts are equally valid ways of knowing, too. They are integral to the human experience, and necessary in trying to apprehend the mystery of who we are, where we came from, and where we might be going. Although not generally as highly valued in our hyper-"technologized" world—where empirical knowledge and scientific method have been enshrined as the one true god—the arts are in fact no less important in understanding and expanding ourselves.

Like the sciences, the arts have their own kinds of procedures—their techniques, symbols, and systems—for judging what is ethically and spiritually revelatory of the human experience, and what indeed is *worth* revealing and building upon in the human experience; what beauty is, and how to create and evaluate it; and how, moreover, through the various artistic media, to capture and extend the range and richness of human subjectivity.

Kant called this kind of knowing "poetic." He asserted that, together, the mathetic and poetic capacities—each with its own visions and vocabularies, each with its own algorithms for exploring and expanding human awareness and goodness—comprise the fullness of intelligence.

Between these two extremes lie other disciplines and discourses that are mixtures of the two.

Psychology, for instance, which ultimately is nothing less than the systematic study of human subjectivity, is a blend of the mathetic and artistic, and is more an art than a science—despite the fact that the corporate masters who control our societies are attempting to turn psychology, and its sister field of education, into mere instruments of conformity and control. Their goal is to transform the individual into an object—a blindly obedient and slavishly efficient worker in the brave new world of the "military-industrial-educational complex" (Cremin, 1988).

However, at their best, the disciplines that comprise the social sciences—sociology, political science, history, cultural anthropology, and so on—move between the poles of the poetic and the mathetic, intuitive and analytical, depending upon the practitioner and her purposes. In this chapter, we wish to look at educational issues in the disciplines and discourses that stretch from the mathetic pole to the in-between zones of the social sciences. In the next chapter, we will deal with education at the poetic pole.

Before proceeding, however, a caveat is in order. One must always be on guard against creating false dichotomies. It is often naïve—not to mention intellectually, emotionally, and ethically dangerous—to see things in black-and-white terms. Reality is usually much more complex than that and is rarely captured—in its impenetrable subtleties and constant transformations—by the binary statement: "Either A or B." Statements that allow "Both A and B (and probably C, D, E, and X, Y, and Z, too)" are usually more accurate and useful.

What is more, it is often the case that if we look closely, we will find that A has elements or characteristics of B, and B has elements or characteristics of A—and that, far from being simple opposites, they are, when looked at from another angle, closely related. Communism and capitalism are cases in point. Although quite opposite in one sense, they are both products of eighteenth-century rationalist philosophy, both systems for "scientifically" organizing a society, and both grounded in the notion that the flow of capital is the core reality of a society. In this respect, communism and capitalism are ideological and historical cousins.

Indeed, from the very different points of view on society that Aristotle takes in his *Politics* or St. Augustine writes from in his *City of God*, communism and capitalism are extremely similar to each other, for neither Marx nor Smith analyzed society in the essentially metaphysical terms that Aristotle or Augustine favored but, instead, rooted their discussions in strictly utilitarian, Enlightenment-philosophy soil. In other words, communism, "A," and capitalism, "B," are opposite in one sense but almost indistinguishable from each other in another.

The same is true of the mathetic and poetic modes of knowing. In one sense, they are clearly opposite. In another sense, they weave and interweave throughout each other so frequently and intricately that it is impossible to tell where one begins and the other leaves off. Mathetic analyses often rely on poetic powers such as intuition, inspiration, imagery, and dreams. The great mathematician Poincare once said that all of his theorems began as images which he then "clothed" with numbers; and Einstein is reputed to have said that his theory of relativity began when he was a boy wondering what it would be like to ride on a beam of light.

Conversely, artistic fruits often arise out of mathetic ground. Some poets claim that what they first "get" in the creative process is a complex set of systematic rhythms that are more or less mathematically regular, and they then flesh these out with words and images to make a poem. And one only need listen to the opening movement of one of Beethoven's final quartets to imagine what a complex, eerily otherworldly calculus would sound like if put to music.

We have separated the poetic and mathetic in this book, however, for two reasons.

First, holistic educational theory has traditionally made a distinction between the academic-rationalist (mathetic) curriculum and the artistic-existential (poetic) one, and we want our discussion to be consistent with the holistic tradition that we subscribe to as scholars and teachers.

Second, it is *pragmatically* useful for the classroom teacher to understand what is *essentially* mathetic and what is *essentially* poetic in order to have a principled way of creating curricula and devising pedagogical strategies that cater to each modality. In short, while there are significant philosophical reasons for understanding the deep interaction of the mathetic and poetic domains, there are also compelling educational reasons for looking at each one separately.

THE PIAGETIAN MODEL OF THE EMERGENCE OF REASON IN THE DEVELOPING CHILD

Over seventy years ago, the Swiss psychologist Jean Piaget offered what is perhaps still the most highly regarded and widely deployed model of the developmental stages that a child goes through from birth until about age twelve in learning to reason. Because it is so broadly and frequently used in educational theory and practice, we will focus upon this model in our discussion of the psychological development of rationality and procedural capabilities in the child.

According to Piaget, the child goes through four stages in the development of reason.[1] They are educationally crucial. If the child is given a task to do or an idea to entertain in the classroom, it should match her present stage of cognitive maturation. This is the core of the idea of *developmentally appropriate* education. To confront a student with something that she is not developmentally prepared to handle will cause her to be frustrated. Conversely, giving her too many things to do or think about in the classroom that she has already developmentally mastered can easily lead to boredom.

When a curriculum is just the right blend of things that the student has mastered and things she does not yet know but is developmentally prepared to handle, then the conditions are optimal for learning. The reader may recall a similar idea from the previous chapter in Krashen's fourth hypothesis about L2 acquisition, the Comprehensible Input Hypothesis.

This states that an individual moves from understanding something in L2 at level X to understanding at the level of X+1 because she is able to comprehend the input that is contained in utterance X, and this forms the basis for her to infer the surplus meaning of X+1, which she does not know, but which she can now gather from context. The general pedagogical point is that there must be a balance of already existing abilities with proximate but not-yet-mastered ones for learning to happen.

Piaget and the Laws of Cognition

Beginning with the sensorimotor stage (birth to eighteen months) and moving on to the second stage, the preoperational one (eighteen months to seven years), the first two rungs on the Piagetian developmental ladder are all about the child's growth as a physical organism encountering other physical objects and organisms. That is to say, the child does not consciously grasp the rules that govern her world of sensations and objects. She is, of course, learning to move through that world of immediate encounter with increasing efficacy—but still without systematic understanding.

This begins to change at the third stage, however, the stage of concrete-operations (seven years to twelve years). This stage is "concrete" in that, like the first two stages, it centers on the child's physical world. However, the quantum leap that the child makes at this stage is that she can perform *operations* on that world. That is to say, she can begin to reason about how the physical world works and how to handle it. In concrete operations (such as striation, sequencing, and conservation, as Piaget called them) the focus is on the child's discovery of the basic laws governing her proximate physical universe.

The next and final stage for Piaget is called formal operations (from about twelve years on). At the earliest substages of formal operations, the child deals with (among other things) the dawning awareness of the ethical codes governing her social world. On this maturational landscape, then, the developmental task is to understand basic physical *rules* and rudimentary social *roles.*

Wilber (2000) thus calls the developmental terrain spanning concrete operations and early formal operations the "rules/roles" landscape—the territory of new kinds of laws, physical and interpersonal. This final developmental stage is most relevant to education from middle-school on. On this culminating landscape beginning about middle school, a person begins to define herself as (for instance) a student at a particular school, a member of a particular religious organization, club, or ethnic or socioeconomic group.

Since early adolescence is seen as the time when this type of self-concept forms, it is also then that a child's peers typically begin to assume increased significance in her life. She begins to see herself through their eyes and her primary psychosocial goal is to shape herself according to the opinions of this "imaginary audience" (Elkind, 1968). Thus, living according to the *mores* of one's primary "reference groups" becomes the premier existential project at this point in life—a project that is social through and through.

The upper regions of formal operations are where the ability to engage in hypothetico-deductive reasoning develops and takes hold. The youth grows increasingly adroit at handling abstract logical propositions. She can picture constructs and systems that do not exist, or do not exist *yet*—and are not tied in to concrete realities, local conditions, or personal affiliations. Interpretive-procedural consciousness often asks "what if" and imagines "as if" in ways that may challenge the student's personal and cultural affiliations.

Part of this ability consists in *metacognition*—the capacity to think about thinking. Formal-operational consciousness observes itself and its social contexts in order to critique and transform them, scrutinizing social and philosophical "givens" that it had previously just accepted at face value.

Interpretive-procedural analyses often take the form of a search for Kant's "categorical imperatives"—those presumably universal ethical principles that anyone can supposedly discover simply by consulting his intuition. Thus, at the very upper regions of formal operations, the ability to formulate cognitive laws begins to merge with the ability to formulate ethical ones. Piaget addressed this in such works as *The Moral Judgment of the Child* (1966). This issue would be taken up in greater depth by Lawrence Kohlberg (1987).

Kohlberg identified three stages of what he called "moral reasoning." In the first stage, "the preconventional," a child "reasons" that something is good or bad depending upon whether it brings her pleasure or pain. In the second stage, "the conventional," the individual reasons that something is good or bad depending upon whether or not it is consistent with the social conventions and norms that define her society. According to Kohlberg, most people never go very far beyond this type of moral reasoning.

A few, however, will move into the upper regions of moral reasoning, the third stage, which he called "post-conventional." At this stage, a person can go beyond the norms of her society in order to arrive at rational, universal principles of right and wrong that, precisely because they are universal, transcend mere cultural norms.

Sometimes a person risks danger, even death, by insisting upon ethical principles that, although not necessarily contradictory to certain social norms, are not rooted in them either and can therefore often seen by the culture as dangerous. This is especially true, of course, when the universal ethical principles *do* run contrary to certain social norms. The classic example of this is Socrates' state execution by the Athenian government because he was thought by the social power-structure to be teaching ethical principles that would lessen young people's sense of loyalty to their society and government.

To return to Piaget, in whose work Kohlberg's is based, following is a brief outline of the major characteristics of each of the stages in Piaget's model.

Stage One: The Sensory-Motor Stage (from birth until about age two): "During this stage, the child learns about himself and his environment through motor and reflex actions. Thought derives from sensation and movement. The child learns that he is separate from his environment and that aspects of his environment—his parents or favorite toy—continue to exist even though they may be outside the reach of his senses. Teaching for a child in this stage should be geared to the sensorimotor system. You can modify behavior by using the senses: a frown, a stern or soothing voice—all serve as appropriate techniques."

Stage Two: The Preoperational Stage (from about two until about seven): "Applying his new knowledge of language, the child begins to use symbols to represent objects. Early in this stage he also personifies objects. He is now better able to think about things and events that are not immediately present. Oriented to the present, the child has difficulty conceptualizing time. His thinking is influenced by fantasy—the way he would like things to be—and he assumes that others see situations from his viewpoint. He takes in information and then changes it in his mind to fit his ideas. Teaching must take into account the child's vivid fantasies and undeveloped sense of time. Using neutral words, body outlines and equipment a child can touch gives him an active role in learning."

Stage Three: The Concrete-Operational Stage (from about seven until about twelve): "During this stage . . . the child develops an ability to think abstractly and to make rational judgments about concrete or observable phenomena, which in the past he needed to manipulate physically to understand."

Stage Four: The Formal-Operational Stage (from about twelve on): "This stage brings cognition to its final form. This person no longer requires concrete objects to make rational judgments. At this point, he is capable of hypothetical and deductive reasoning. Teaching for the adolescent may be wide-ranging because he will be able to consider many possibilities from several perspectives" ("Piaget's Cognitive Stages," Springhouse Corporation. Retrieved January 11, 2010, at http://honolulu.hawaii.edu/intranet/committees/FacDevCom/guidebk/teachtip/piaget.htm). It is the student at this final stage, formal operations, who is the focus of this chapter.

Although Piaget's model is still felt to be fundamentally sound by many developmental psychologists, it has nevertheless been critiqued on various grounds (Crain, 1992).

Some critics point to Piaget's lack of adequate attention to how "reason" is differentially defined and employed in different cultures. In other words, what people consider reasonable, and what they consider it reasonable to do with that "reasonable" knowledge, may vary widely across cultures, and even within cultures (Rogoff, 2003). Still others criticize Piaget for his apparent assumption that reason emerges in a social vacuum, in the same stages and rhythms for all people everywhere, according to universal laws that are simply inherent in the human being *per se*, as is the case in puberty or menopause, for example (Vygotsky, 1986).

Additionally, certain feminist psychologists accuse the model of a revolving around a "male" bias in defining what "reason" is and how to "appropriately" employ it. The idea here is that men tend to define what is reasonable abstractly, in the form of universal laws and other codified standards that are more or less *context-free*—that is to say, without regard to whom the individuals in a situation specifically are or what their particular challenges, strengths, and needs might be.

On the other hand, women tend to believe that no solution to a problem is truly reasonable unless it nurtures the individuals involved in the problem, and does so in a way that is *context-sensitive*—i.e., finely attuned to who each individual uniquely is, which, by definition, the gross generalities of a mere codicillary approach to justice can never do (Belenky et al., 1986; Gilligan, 1982).

Another line of criticism of Piaget's model challenges his premise that an individual must "unitarily" move from Stage A to B—not parts of his developmental potentials in Stage A moving to Stage B at one time and other parts moving from Stage A to B at another time, but entirely from A to B at once.

Included in this critique is the calling into question of Piaget's assumption that a person must move from Stage A to B not only unitarily but in an *invariant* sequence—A to B, B to C, C to D, and so on—whereas, in fact, a person may move, partially or unitarily, from Stage A to C and skip over B, or recycle back at a later date to "do" Stage B or perhaps just "to pick up" parts of B while mostly developing at that point in the domain of Stage C, or D, or Y or Z (Wilber, 2000).

A final criticism focuses on Piaget's apparent belief that rationality is the summit of human consciousness. As important as the ability to reason unquestionably is in the ascent of consciousness, it is clearly a bias of the Western scientific worldview to conclude that it is necessarily the highest or most powerful form of consciousness.

There are also *transrational* (which must not be confused with *irrational*) ways of seeing the world, and seeing *beyond* the world, that must be accounted for in any existentially complete view of human consciousness (Ferrer, 2002). These forms of knowing—including ethical intuition, ontological presence, artistic passion, and mystical revelation—cannot simply be dismissed as marginal and lesser states of awareness and being. Indeed, they may well be higher states of awareness and being.

It is simply counterintuitive and philosophically indefensible to assume, as not only Piaget but most Western developmentalists do, that the evolution of human consciousness somehow "maxes out" with the capacity to think rationally, and that this development is pretty much complete when a person is twelve years old—and that the rest of her life is just a refining of rationality. (In the next chapter, we will look at the educational implications of existential and transrational philosophies.)

These are all important critiques, which the authors share, of not only Piaget's model but of the view that prevails in so much psychological and educational theory and practice that "reason" is universal, free of interpersonal and cultural influences, and the apex of human awareness.

However, it is also true that, whatever else we are, we are, as Aristotle said, the animals that reason. The development of this capacity is crucial psychosocially, ethically, and educationally—and Piaget's model of how reason develops is (keeping the above caveats in mind) still one of the best overall paradigms of how it happens. The Piagetian model is therefore useful to the teacher as a rule-of-thumb in knowing how to forge developmentally appropriate curricula and pedagogically effective strategies with students at a particular age.

METACOGNITION: THE EMERGENCE OF THE STUDENT AS A COGNITIVE APPRENTICE

One of the most exciting things about the formal-operations student is that she is not only now evidencing the capacity to think rationally; she is also demonstrating an ability *to think rationally about thinking rationally*. She is able to reflect on her cognitive processes and ask herself "What does it *mean* to think? And what does it *mean* to think rationally?" She is also learning to think rationally about the *different ways* of thinking rationally in different disciplines. Thus, she might continue her self-examination with the following questions: "What makes thinking in physics so different from thinking in sociology? Each seems rational to me, but each also seems to have its own special way of *being* rational. What makes these two types of rational thinking so different?" To be able to think about thinking, and, specifically, to be able to think about how people think and "proceed" in various disciplines, is called *metacognition*. Metacognition is cognition about cognition. Beginning to think more acutely and self-consciously about what it means to think in the first place, the metacognitive student is learning how to use rational thought—and different types of it—more purposefully and self-consciously. This allows her to formulate valid intellectual goals that she can now attain more efficiently.

The metacognitive student is increasingly able to take a bird's eye view of any mathetic or quasi-mathetic field.[2] She does not now simply memorize facts and a few theories in, say, biology, but is becoming increasingly aware of the implicit assumptions and rules that *govern* how one *thinks* in and goes about *doing* biology. She is experiencing a dawning but compelling awareness of how biology is essentially different from other fields because of its unique assumptions and procedures, all fitting together to make a certain kind of cognitive tool called "biology."

What is more, she is able to formulate and articulate with increasing precision what the basic perspectives and procedures in biology are that differentiate it from another discipline (even though there may, of course, be overlap with hybrid disciplines like biochemistry, biophysics, biostatistics, or psychobiology).

Increasingly able to isolate and examine a discipline's assumptions, procedures, terms, and purposes, she is able to see and say how this field *works*; how its components all fit together to form a particular discipline—a particular *community of discourse*. In this way, the student grows increasingly able to enter the formal conversation of rational academic discourse in a field (Noddings, 1995).

In practical terms, she begins to see that the field of biology is more than just a compilation of facts and concepts to learn—like any other facts and concepts except that these are about living organisms. She can now do more than that. She can begin to see, in a principled way, that biology is a unique *lens* on reality, a unified way of seeing and influencing a particular aspect of the world—a unique *system* of defining, exploring, and shaping existence. She is learning how to *do* biology as a biologist would.

Of course, she will not do it as proficiently as a professional biologist. But as she has more and more experience of understanding biology from the metaperspective of a biologist, and of engaging in the procedures of biological inquiry in a rule-governed, self-reflective, and goal-oriented fashion, she does indeed become more and more like a biologist in her cognition. She is becoming a *cognitive apprentice* in a *community of discourse* (Brown, Collins, & Duguid, 1988).

THE *PROCEDURAL* CURRICULUM

Curricula that focus on developing these skills and dispositions in students have been portrayed in curriculum theory by different names: the "academic-rationalist" curriculum (Eisner & Vallance, 1985), the "intellectual-academic" curriculum (Ornstein & Hunkins, 1988), and the "cognitive-processes" approach (Miller, 1988). All of these rubrics convey the idea that this domain of education revolves around traditional academic disciplines—their languages and logics.

By whatever name they go, in such curricula the scientific method is often held up as offering the best guidance in showing the student to think rationally by: "1) becoming aware of a difficulty (or a felt difficulty), 2) identifying the problem, 3) assembling and classifying data and formulating hypotheses, 4) accepting or rejecting the tentative hypotheses, and 5) formulating conclusions and evaluating them" (Miller, 1988, p. 126). This classical view in conceptual change theory of how to instruct the formal operations student was best outlined in a famous essay by Posner and his associates in 1982.

Posner claimed that there is—or should be—a similarity in how students and scientists change their thinking about something. In both cases, he asserted, the individual's "knowledge claims" and "beliefs" will change to deal with "anomalies" and "contradictory evidence" that a previous paradigm could not handle.

In this model of conceptual change, Posner averred that a student would change her idea about something if: 1) she was dissatisfied with an existing conception because it failed to account for new evidence; 2) she found the new conception that the teacher offered intelligible; 3) she found the new conception plausible; and 4) further experience proved the new conception to be fruitful. To promote procedural learning, therefore, the teacher should look to the scientific method as her model.[3]

But in a deeper sense, the metacognitive student is asked to do more than just evaluate the plausibility of a piece of evidence. She is more fundamentally challenged to ask and answer questions about the discipline/discourse itself: *Is the present piece of evidence manageable given the conceptual structures and investigative methods of this discipline as it presently stands? Or does the evidence present such challenges to the current structures and methods that it requires a rethinking of those structures or methods?*

These are the kinds of inquiries that require higher-order mathetic thinking, for they are not merely empirical questions requiring a one-shot, practical solution to a certain problem. Indeed, such evidence can often go right to the heart of how a discipline is presently structured if that evidence cannot be satisfactorily handled by the discipline as it is presently constituted. This is especially true when the datum is clearly anomalous—strange, and more or less outside the boundaries of the discourse as it is currently structured.

As William James put it, it is not necessary to examine all swans to demonstrate that not all swans are white. Just sighting one black swan will do the trick. One bit of anomalous evidence can cause a system to have to be thought out again—and more or less restructured.

Therefore, metacognitive pedagogies often stress the importance of exposing students to anomalous data. This requires students to take metaperspectives, viewing a system or discipline—or part of it at least—as a whole to see what might need to be changed in that system or discipline in order to account for the anomaly. After that, in true scientific-method fashion, they can test and, if necessary, further revise their conceptual paradigms in order to account for the anomaly. The result of this process is then considered to be procedurally defensible, "true" knowledge. However, it is only true until further notice—until, that is, the appearance of another anomaly that starts the metacognitive process up all over again.

We saw in the previous chapters that cognition is "hot"—radiating with all sorts of passionate personal emotions and pointed political commitments. The procedural curriculum is, in a sense, a salutary attempt to *cool down* the processes of cognition, to help the student "detach" from psychodynamic forces and affiliative causes that might be blinding her to how things really are in the world—not simply how she *feels* they are, or should be, in order to satisfy her emotional needs or further the interests of her cultural reference groups.

This dawning ability in a student to—to some extent—"stand outside" her personal issues and cultural affiliations is what can make her so delightful to her teachers at this stage—and so exasperating to her parents.

The student, learning to critique her previously unquestioned commitments, can now *relativize* them in the light of other and equally defensible ideas and practices. This sometimes drives her parents more than a little crazy as she seems to be cavalierly throwing about and shattering virtually everything they have tried to teach her—casting the parents' belief systems into radical doubt. But this is simply the way things must be if the child is to emerge as an effective critical thinker and to establish herself as an independent adult.

And as we saw in the previous chapter, this is also why it is sometimes hard for a student to emerge as a critical thinker; doing so may require that she interrogate principles and practices that are sacrosanct to her parents but that she now sees as relative to (and not necessarily better than or even as good as) other principles and practices. Some students are—quite understandably—not (yet) willing to make this leap into conceptual hyperspace, leaving their parents behind.

As Pascal said, "The heart has its reasons of which reason knows nothing," and the heart has few attachments that are as compelling as family and culture. The teacher of the procedural curriculum must understand that it is not always a cognitive inadequacy but may well be a personal commitment that causes a student to reject, or only partially accept, the teacher's "rational" pronouncements.

THE STUDENT AS A COGNITIVE APPRENTICE

The formal-operational student, armed with metacognition, is ready to become a "cognitive apprentice" (Brown, Collins, & Duguid, 1988). This means that she is developmentally capable of taking the first real steps, however small, in entering a community of discourse that is comprised of "master practitioners" in that field. If she decides to enter that community of discourse more deeply, even to the extent of making it her professional focus, she must, like any apprentice, learn to use tools (conceptual tools, of course, but sometimes physical ones as well, as in the case of surgery) as masters in the field use them. If she is particularly gifted and lucky, she may someday be able to go beyond the masters in not only using their established tools but in creating new ones.

As she proves her competence, first with a classroom teacher in the school years, and ultimately under the watchful eyes of established experts in the field in her university years and beyond, she becomes more firmly embedded and perhaps even more widely known in that community of thinkers and practitioners. She becomes more adept at using its language, more conversant with the rules that govern its modes of inquiry, more practiced in the various roles that one can play within that community, and more aware of which roles suit her interests and talents best.

She incrementally attains to higher levels of credentialing within the field that confer more credibility upon her and provide her with richer resources to pursue her path in that intellectual community. In short, in moving step by step up the ladder from novice to expert, the student is, like an apprentice in any field, basically learning *how to be a member of a culture*—in this case, a culture of procedural experts in a certain discipline. She is becoming acculturated.

This pedagogy—that sees the student as a cognitive apprentice—began with the great cognitive psychologist and instructional theorist Jerome Bruner in the 1960s. It has been called a "Structure-of-the-Discipline" theory of education (Bruner, 1960) because, in Bruner's view, the classroom teacher, by both explicit instruction and implicit modeling, should show students how to define and solve problems in a given discipline and thereby become familiar with its structure.

In this manner, students learn how experts in that field do their work.[4] Some educational researchers have gone so far as to "draw" cognitive maps that are supposed to represent how experts in a field see and solve a given problem. The pedagogical objective is to get students to reshape their internal cognitive maps of that problem until it more or less conforms to that of the expert" (Chi, Feltovich, & Glaser, 1981).

Unlike Piaget, Bruner believed that this could happen at virtually any grade level as long as the curriculum and instruction were developmentally appropriate to the student's present stage and the teacher had enough of a grasp of a discipline to at least introduce her students to its basic components. When the student reached a sufficient level of expertise (and this, of course, could not begin to happen until she had developmentally entered formal operations) she might then begin to continue her studies in the field from experts in the field—usually at the university level and beyond.

But at whatever level, from the earliest grades to doctoral studies, Bruner insisted that the "structure of knowledge" in a discipline should form the foundation for teaching students about the discipline. What he called the discipline's "mode of representation, economy, and power" needed to be adapted to the capacities of a particular developmental and/or ability group. He wrote:

> Any idea or problem or body of knowledge can be presented in a form simple enough so that any particular learner can understand it in a recognizable form. The structure of any domain of knowledge may be characterized in three ways, each affecting the ability of any learner to master it: the *mode of representation* in which it is put, its *economy*, and its effective *power*. Mode, economy, and effective power vary in relation to different ages, to different "styles" among learners, and to different subject matters. Any domain of knowledge (or any problem within a domain of knowledge) can be represented in three ways: by a set of actions for achieving a certain result (enactive representation); by a set of summary images or graphics that stand for a concept without defining it fully (iconic representation); and by a set of symbolic and logical propositions drawn from a symbolic system that is governed by rules or laws for forming and transforming propositions (symbolic representation). (Bruner, 1960, pp. 44–48)

In sum, the best curricula in any domain are developmentally appropriate ones, share the domain's assumptions, mirror its structures, and employ its processes to approach problems that are typical in that domain. This helps the student to some degree—and a greater and greater one as the student matures—to assume the role of a practitioner in that particular domain. This process begins to swing into full gear with the advent of metacognition.

Bruner even developed an anthropology curriculum, *Man: A Course of Study*, that translated this theory into practice in teaching students not merely various facts and ideas from anthropology but how to *think* like anthropologists do.

The so-called "New Math" of the 1960s also exemplifies Bruner's theories. The New Math infuriated many parents because it was unlike the traditional way of learning math that the parents had known in their school years. Instead of just "plugging" numbers into already devised formulas and handily "chugging out" answers (the famous "plug n' chug" approach to math), the new approach was to try to get students to grasp the reasoning behind the formulas so that, to some extent, the students could "come up" with those formulas on their own, or at least get an intuitive *sense* of how the mathematicians themselves had done so.

This new way of teaching often involved all kinds of new symbols and procedures—some of them drawn from the field of formal logic—that mystified parents who, faced with strange Greek letters and even stranger graphics, suddenly had no idea of how to help their children with math homework; these tasks now had more to do with developing procedural insights into math and less to do with the actual numerical "correctness" of an answer to a problem.

Numerical correctness was still important, of course, but even more important than mechanically writing the correct answer to a problem on the page was understanding *why* that answer was correct and *how* that answer was ultimately illustrative of the way mathematicians work.[5]

The specific form of procedurally sensitive curriculum varies according to the history, worldview, and objectives of that specific discipline. It means one thing in terms of curriculum and instruction to help a student see the world like a physicist and quite another to help her see the world like a historian. The structure of the procedurally centered curriculum will also vary according to the inclinations and objectives of the teacher—not to mention her degree of familiarity with the discipline.

But whatever the community of discourse that a student is being inducted into, Bruner felt that it is the generally accepted perspectives, standard procedures, determining texts, and specific discourse of the discipline that should drive instruction. And as a student became more metacognitively adept, the curriculum should more closely mirror the actual discipline itself until finally the student would enter the discipline as a full-fledged cognitive apprentice, a "master in the making."

The popular view of becoming a master in an academic field is one in which a student memorizes all the most important facts and theories in a discipline and then regurgitates them on a test until she passes enough tests to become a master herself. This view of the academic process is too often all too true among staid or lazy academics who are happy with the intellectual *status quo* and their old lecture notes that they do not want to have to redo! However, real masters in a field have a deeper vision of their field. It goes far beyond the limited view of it as a static body of invariant facts and unquestionable theories.

Rather, the real master sees her field as a dynamic conversation among adepts who, motivated by passionate curiosity and a kind of divine discontent with any merely "settled" knowledge, are constantly trying to expand the intellectual and ethical reaches of their field. They carry this project to the nth degree, periodically redefining their field through asking ever more compelling questions, engaging in ever more radical ways of engaging those questions, and striving for ever more elegant theories.

In a sense, a true master in a field is not one who rests content in knowledge as if it were a mansion, but, rather, one who uses present knowledge as a vehicle to go to new places and entertain new questions of expanding charm and deeper consequence.

LIPMAN'S PHILOSOPHY OF THE CURRICULUM: PHILOSOPHY *AS* CURRICULUM

In this section we will focus on the curriculum theory of Matthew Lipman because we feel it represents one of the best approaches to the procedural curriculum. This is because of its general applicability across various disciplines and its ethical focus on what it means to be a reasonable person in a pluralistic democracy.

Lipman, Philosophy, and the Child

According to Lipman, schools everywhere have fallen short because teachers and administrators have not turned classrooms into communities of rational discourse. Lipman proclaims that "as educators, we have a heavy responsibility for the unreasonableness of the world's population" (1988, p. 250). "The greatest disappointment of traditional education has been its failure to produce people approximating the ideal of reasonableness" (p. 251).

The "socially patterned defects" that contaminate education have to be eradicated, Lipman believes, by an aggressive campaign to make the power to reason the center of all curricula. This entails "bringing a greater degree of order into the curriculum, into the methodology of teaching, into the process of teacher education, and into the procedures of testing" (p. 252).

Mirroring Bruner's view that even the youngest children can think procedurally, Lipman believes that teachers can remedy the failures of traditional education by bringing philosophy into even the earliest grades of the schools. "Even young children can enter into such dialogue," asserts Lipman, for "doing philosophy is not a matter of age but of ability to reflect scrupulously and courageously on what one finds important" (p. 249). That reflection, which includes "classical rhetoric and dialectic," is suitable even for young children as long as they are "given practice in discussing the *concepts* they take seriously" (p. 249, emphasis added).

Not only is such instruction possible, even at the earlier levels—it is necessary, so necessary, in fact, that it should become "the core or armature of the curriculum" (p. 249). "Because philosophy is the discipline that best prepares us to think in terms of the other disciplines, it must be assigned a central role in the early as well as in the late stages of the educational process" (p. 252).

Of the thirty critical skills that Lipman wants students to acquire, he feels that the ability to work with the following is the most important: "(1) concepts; (2) generalizations; (3) cause-effect relationships; (4) consistencies and contradictions; (5) analogies; (6) part-whole and whole-part connections; (7) problem formulations; (8) reversibility of logical statements; and (9) application of principles to real-life situations" (Ornstein & Hunkins, 1988, p. 98).

Thinking *reasonably* also means thinking *creatively*. It means using the imagination to envision new worlds. Yet, this is something that the student will never fully do, Lipman reminds us, if she is forced to consider issues that she feels are personally and socially irrelevant. This notion brings us to the Progressive pedagogies of the early twentieth century in the United States. Like Dewey, whom Lipman acknowledges as central to his pedagogy, Lipman insists that emotionally and politically significant and lasting types of learning can only occur in classrooms where the individual's cognition is situated in a community of learners engaged in interesting tasks. Students will not truly learn or long remember things that do not interest them or relate to their lives.

As did Dewey (1916), Lipman hopes that restructuring schooling so as to focus on rationality and procedural skills will ultimately work massive social transformations.

> There is good reason to think that the model of each and every classroom—that which it seeks to approximate and at times becomes—is the community of inquiry. By inquiry, of course, I mean perseverance in self-corrective exploration of issues that are felt to be both important and problematic. . .If we begin with the practice in the classroom—the practice of converting it into a reflective community that thinks in the disciplines about the world and about its thinking about the world, we soon come to recognize that communities can be nested within larger communities and these within larger communities still, if all hold the same allegiance to the same procedure of inquiry. There is the familiar ripple effect outward, like the stone thrown in the pond: wider and wider, more and more encompassing communities are formed, each commu-

nity consisting of individuals committed to self-corrective exploration and creativity. (Lipman, 1988, p. 252)

Lipman's theory beautifully satisfies the requirements of the procedural curriculum, which are that a curriculum should involve rich conversation, be rational and active, and foster cognitive processes in helping to create and maintain a just society.

CULTURE, REASON, AND RHETORIC

As we have seen, inducting a student into a community of discourse naturally involves a great deal of conversation in the classroom—between the teacher and student, among the students, and with the texts that are the launching pads from which so much classroom discussion takes off. In such a radically pluralistic society as ours, therefore, it is well for the teacher in any educational setting, from the kindergarten room to the doctoral seminar, to know that different cultural groups tend to favor different conversational styles.

An awareness of this fact enables the teacher to accommodate various modes of processing and communicating ideas. Not only does this create an inclusive pedagogy in which a wide range of discursive styles are honored in the classroom, thereby creating a warm and inviting environment in which all students feel comfortable participating in their own ways. It also exposes students to new ways of inquiring and communicating the results of those inquiries. This enriches everyone. It adds to each student's armamentarium of cognitive strategies for seeing, being, and doing in the world.

The following graphic symbolizes the results of a great deal of research on different discursive styles, each of which tends to be favored by certain cultural groups. Here, of course, as always when talking about cultural proclivities, the key phrase is "tends to." As valuable as these generalizations are, they must always be used with caution, understanding that any student in a culture may favor other perspectives and enactments than those that typify her culture.

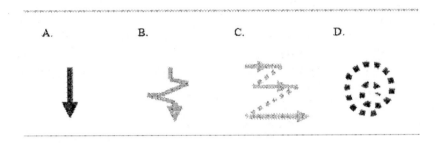

Figure 4.1

The first culturally conditioned rhetorical pattern, A, is what is called the "Anglo-Germanic" rhetorical style. The reader will immediately recognize this pattern, no doubt, as the one that is most common in the discourse of the typical classroom. Its features include:

1. "linear logic, thinking in straight lines, rather than more lateral or spiral logics of other traditions;
2. an analytical approach that emphasizes dividing reality into its component parts, rather than more synthetic approaches that emphasize the whole over the parts;
3. an expository, declarative, and deductive rhetorical style that works from the 'big picture' or thesis statement down through the supporting details or arguments, rather than an inductive style that requires learners to be more tentative, stating rationales and arguments before attempting a more generalized statement;
4. debate, discussion, and original thinking, compared with academic traditions such as that which Robinson (1999) describes for Chinese learners, for whom three key rules are 'memorize the lesson, practice the skill, and respect superiors.'
5. the written over the spoken word. Despite the continuing dominance of the lecture as the teaching mode, learners in the West are assessed primarily on their ability to express themselves in written form. In contrast, most of the world's languages have only recently been written down" (Spronk, 2004).

As powerful as this discourse pattern is, it is not the only way of having conversations in the classroom. Other patterns are equally powerful and each has its own specific strengths.

Discourse pattern B, for instance, which typifies the Romance languages (Spanish, French, Italian, Portuguese, and Romanian—so called because they are from Latin, and hence "Roman," and not necessarily because they are more "romantic" than any other languages) moves from introduction to conclusion no less certainly than pattern A.

In Latinate discourse, however, there is less of a "hurry" to get from beginning to conclusion. Illustrative anecdotes and spontaneous musings, flashes of unplanned and perhaps still rather tenuous insights, and, in short, lots of creative "rambling around" the conversational territory to see what might emerge in the course of the conversational journey—these are what are prized in Romance discourse. While Pattern A is admirable in its economy and speed, Pattern B also offers a great deal in terms of personal and poetic enrichment of the topics under discussion.

Pattern C illustrates Semitic discourse—Hebrew and Arabic. Here, the discursive pattern is chiastic—that is, a theme is stated, illustrated by various points, and then restated, before the speaker embarks on the next topic. The focus is on dramatic repetition and parallelism. The great appeal of this discursive mode is its ability to plant an idea in the listener's mind, adorn it with an array of compelling examples, slightly variant cases, and further thoughts that add enormous subtlety to the original proposition and thereby lend, it, by the time it is restated, a resonance, richness, and mystery that go beyond what the first proposition communicated.

Finally, Pattern D, the Asian discourse pattern, is one in which the speaker and listeners circumambulate a topic, "mosey" around it—seeing it from many angles, not necessarily committing themselves to any particular perspective (at least not yet), and generously entertaining many people's views on the topic under analysis before beginning to try to put them all together in one grand, "synthetic" solution if possible. The sum of such discourse is much greater than merely the number of its parts, for in this way of examining and talking about something, the various perspectives can bootstrap each other onto higher ground than any one perspective could have ever reached by itself.

Each style also has its limitations: A can be cold, pushy, and sterile. B can be filled with so many digressions that one loses sight of what the conversation was about in the first place, and no useful conclusions are reached. C can be simply repetitive—dull and soporific. And D can be so accommodating of so many perspectives that the conclusions, although not "offending" anybody, also do not establish anything, and thus, wishy-washy, do not lead to any particularly useful ideas for further discussion or any game-plans for concrete action.

Another culturally variable rhetorical difference is between what is called "*topic-centered*" and "*topic-chaining*" speaking and writing (Gay, 2000, pp. 95-97). Topic-centered discourse is factual and linear. Topic-chaining discourse is anecdotal, spontaneous, poetic, and personal. Topic-centered discourse keeps discussion on task and economical. It is rich in the empirical and analytical functions. Topic-chaining discourse is flexible and poetic. Its strength lies in its ability to intuit and feel deeply.

Another important distinction that is often made regarding cognitive styles comes from the field of Gestalt psychology: "Discrete-point/analytical" cognition (sometimes called "field independence") versus "holistic/relational" cognition ("field independence").

"Discrete-point/analytical" people prefer isolating details and then putting them together to create a pattern in a step-by-step, rule-governed manner. At the opposite extreme, "holistic/relational" people favor taking a situation in in an intuitive, emotionally charged flash—in the context of which they then begin to examine specific details in relation to that whole picture. Field independent people work from facts to patterns. Field dependent people work from patterns to facts.

> Global [holistic] processing emphasizes the whole and the relationships between its parts (e.g., whole language, sight word vocabulary building.) Analytic [discrete point] processing emphasizes processing individual parts and gradually building the whole in a *carefully controlled sequence* (e.g., phonics, sounding out words). Other terms for global are simultaneous, holistic, relational. Analytic processing is usually sequential and ordered. (More, 1986, p. 154; emphasis added).

Why are topic-sequencing and field-orientation cultural issues? Because there is considerable evidence of a relationship between culture and processing styles.[6] The relationship is by no means absolute in the sense that a person from Culture A will inevitably be field independent while a person from Culture B will necessarily be field dependent, but there are statistical tendencies that have been observed which indicate that there are *degrees of probability* that a person from Culture A will *tend* to be either field dependent or field independent.

In a classroom where all discourse styles are honored, they can enrich and help to "correct" each other, thus maximizing the yield of any academic discussion by offering multiple perspectives on a topic or issue. As in Cubist painting, where the artist's intent was to allow the viewer to see a single subject from various perspectives simultaneously, multiple perspectives on a topic or issue in the classroom engenders what the Existentialist educational philosopher Maxine Greene (1974) called a Cubist curriculum.

The rhetorician Kenneth Burke once said that "every way of seeing is also a way of not seeing" (Burke, 1989, p. 63). With the opportunity to see in so many different ways, the student in the discursively diverse classroom can increase her sight and insights many times over, learning how to *be* and *act* in the world in ways that may never have occurred to her before but which now become part of her store of cognitive and lifestyle possibilities both in the classroom and out.

CONCLUSION

In speaking of the procedural curriculum, it is best to talk not so much about "rationality" as about "rationalities." There are many systematic ways of knowing, growing, and showing in the world. Each way constitutes an existential procedure for interpreting and acting upon self, other, society, and nature. When one of those ways assumes the status of an academic "approach," then we can call it a "discipline." Disciplines vary because our perspectives on and purposes in our lives are so variable, as is the world with which we are dealing.

There is also variability in how different groups of people—who are joined together either by birth, location, history, or preference—go about seeing and being in the world. To bring these different disciplines—and these different cultural perspectives *on* those disciplines—into more exciting, compassionate, and productive interaction is the challenge and promise for not only the teacher of the procedural curriculum but indeed for everyone in the rapidly shifting conceptual landscapes of the multicultural twenty-first century.

APPLICATION: THE PROCEDURAL DIMENSION

The Procedural Dimension for curriculum provides opportunities for students to inquire systematically into the various disciplines and related discourse of each of the content areas. Through the Procedural Dimension, students can come to know both the science and art of the disciplines by functioning as cognitive apprentices. As apprentices, students engage in the disciplines in the same manner as members of the related communities of practice do. Following are two examples of such learning processes.

FRAMEWORK FOR COMPREHENSIVE MATHEMATICS INSTRUCTION (CMI)

Walter, Peterson, Ridlon, and Hilton (2004) developed the framework for Comprehensive Mathematics Instruction (CMI) in order help students deepen and broaden their mastery of mathematics. Using the framework for CMI, teachers engage students in inquiry-based processes that mathematicians use to identify, frame, and solve problems. From these processes, students learn to think like mathematicians and develop insight into how mathematics is uniquely different from other content areas, while at the same time it can also be a thread that runs through them.

The CMI framework consists of three phases of inquiry-based learning: Develop Understanding, Solidify Understanding, and Practice Understanding (Walter et al., 2004). According to Walter and his colleagues (2004), the goal for Develop Understanding is to surface student thinking, which contributes to their understanding of ideas, strategies, and representations relative to a particular mathematical purpose. For Solidify Understanding, the goal is to help students develop mathematical concepts, algorithms, and tools by examining and extending student ideas, strategies, and representations. The goal of Practice Understanding is to facilitate students' development of definitions and properties, procedures, and models by refining and acquiring fluency with concepts, algorithms, and tools. Within each of these learning phases, students are engaged in Launching, Exploring, and Discussing mathematical tasks.

Teachers position students to function as cognitive apprentices as they co-construct mathematical understanding with their classmates and teachers, alternately serving as learners, coaches, and teachers. The CMI process will be illustrated by an example taken from a study conducted by Tiffany Marie Hessing (2006) in which she investigated *Second Graders' Solution Strategies and Understanding of a Combination Mathematical Problem.*

This example of CMI instruction will be taken from the Develop Understanding phase and will be described in terms of three stages: launch, explore, and discuss.

Launch. The teacher initiated student learning by posing a task that had a clear mathematical purpose with multiple paths to solutions and/or multiple solutions and was aligned with a state or national standard or objective. The task was carefully phrased so students could use many different approaches to engage in the task. In this example the focus of the task was mathematical combining. Hessing (2006) recorded the task the teacher introduced to her students as follows: "Emily has three shirts. One is blue, one is yellow and one is red. She also has two pairs of pants. One is green and one is black. How many different outfits can she make?" (p. 15)

Explore. The teacher provided students with squares that represented the colors of Emily's three shirts and two pants in order to facilitate students' thinking. As part of the exploration, students surfaced ideas, developed problem-solving strategies, and built visual representations using colored squares, drawings, charts, colored tiles and so forth. To facilitate student discourse and exploration, the teacher moved around the room asking individuals and small groups of students' questions that caused them to clarify and deepen their mathematical thinking. In this stage, the teacher identified three to five ideas to share during the discussion phase—some that illustrated correct thinking and others that reflected flawed thinking.

Discuss. Prior to the whole group discussion, students worked in pairs to present their visual representations of the problem and explain their reasoning. The teacher strategically invited three to five students to present their visual representation of the combination problem and the strategies they used to reason the problem out to the whole group. The teacher orchestrated a discussion of selected features of the presenters' visual representations and reasoning. At the conclusion of the lesson the teacher asked students if the task was an addition problem, which spurred another flurry of productive thinking and mathematical reasoning.

Students functioned as cognitive apprentices in a community of learners by collectively solving a task that focused on the reasoning of mathematical combinations. Students constructed mathematical understanding by making visual representations, presenting mathematical propositions, and posing questions. Talking as fellow mathematicians, students engaged in mathematical discourse; they posed questions, challenged each others' propositions, and defended their thinking. Through this process, the classroom shifted from being teacher centered with students turning to the teacher to ask questions and expecting explanations to being student-centered with students asking questions, giving explanations, coaching, and teaching each other.

READING SHARE

The intended outcome of the Reading Share as presented by Sharon Taberisky (2008) is to help students come to know themselves as readers and to help them develop into strategic and proficient readers. The Reading Share is held at the end of each period of independent self-selected reading. The teacher facilitates this reflective process by inviting students to sit together in a cozy group around a large comfortable rocker.

Teachers encourage students to reflect on themselves as readers with this question, "Students, what did you learn about yourself today as a reader?" Individual students who answer sit on the rocker (a position of power) surrounded by peers to share insights they have gleaned about themselves as readers. Once their insights are presented, the teacher asks them probing questions that invite deeper thinking and paraphrases what they said so they can hear their thinking. Peers are also invited to make comments or ask questions about students' insights.

Following is a sample dialogue from the work of Sharon Taberiski (2008) with a second grader to whom we will refer as Nancy, who is sharing insights into herself as a reader:

Nancy: "Today I learned that it is better to read silently in my head rather than reading the words out loud."

Teacher (probing): "Why is it important to read silently in your head?"

Nancy: "Because when you read the words out loud you read more slowly and it takes you longer to read the book."

Teacher (paraphrasing): "Oh, so you think it is faster to read silently in your head than reading out loud?"

Josh (peer): "Also, if you read out loud, you can disturb other kids who are trying to concentrate on their books, but when you read in your head, you don't disturb anyone."

Teacher (paraphrasing): "So reading silently in your head not only helps you read faster, but it also doesn't disturb other students who are reading."

Being able to articulate these insights not only builds self-awareness for the student who shares, but also spreads the wisdom to students throughout the class. One could accurately predict that many students who heard that reflective dialogue would self-monitor their own independent reading and intentionally form the habit of reading silently in order to read more quickly and to avoid interfering with other students' concentration. Likely, this strategy of reading silently would come up in subsequent reading shares as other students discover its power for themselves.

Through this reflective and dialogic process, the strategy of reading silently would come to light more powerfully and would likely be embraced more deeply by more students than if the teacher had simply relied on telling students to read silently. Furthermore, students would develop a sense of empowerment and self-knowledge through this process as they are encouraged to share more of their thinking through the teacher's gentle probes and to hear their thinking reflected back to them by the teacher's paraphrases and their peers' comments.

By reflecting together, students would likely build shared knowledge about the reading process and gather an array of strategies from which they can choose to enhance their reading strategically. Students would also likely build a shared ethos of viewing reading as an important skill that they can continuously refine together. Likely, students will learn the importance of learning with and from each other, trusting their thinking to one another as a community of reading practitioners who are endeavoring to increase their reading prowess.

While this example has focused on a second-grade classroom, this Reading Share (Taberiski, 2008) is also valuable for older students as they reflect on themselves as readers of self-selected books during independent reading.

NOTES

1. Each stage has a number of substages in Piaget's model but these need not concern us here.

2. Of course, a student at this stage can also become metacognitive in terms of poetic cognition, too—not only writing a poem, for instance, but trying to understand at deeper and in more systematic ways what it means to write a poem at all. We will deal with poetic metacognition in the next chapter.

3. Whether or not scientists *actually* think and carry on their research in such a tidy, step-by-step fashion has been called into question by philosophers of science, many of whom feel that scientific discovery is a much more intuitive, even poetic, activity than the popular image of the coldly dispassionate scientist in her white lab coat would suggest. Still, this popular notion of scientific inquiry is implicit in many procedural curricula, especially in the so-called "hard sciences." See Kuhn, *The Structure of Scientific Revolutions,* 1970.

4. Research into teacher thinking over the last several decades has shown, however, how often and how widely the classroom teacher's understanding of a discipline differs from the expert's understanding of it.

5. Interestingly, there were also political motivations behind the development of this pedagogy, which arose in the context of the Cold War. It was felt that the United States was falling, or would soon fall, behind the Soviet Union in producing the scientists and mathematicians who would provide a country with the conceptual tools and actual hardware necessary to prevail in the Cold War. Not surprisingly, then, it was math, physics, and foreign languages (since foreign languages were indispensable to espionage) that received the greatest attention and experienced the most curricular restructuring during this time. See Cremin, 1988; Spring, *The Sorting Machine,* 1976; Tyack, 1974.

6. For an analysis of culturally variable rhetorical/cognitive styles and their educational significance, see Mayes et al., 2007, *Understanding the Whole Student: Holistic Multicultural Education.*

Chapter Five

The Existential Dimension

We are beings who seek meaning. A person is more than just the sum total of the factors that impinge upon him at every moment in the physical, psycho-dynamic, cultural, and cognitive realms. As crucial as these determinants are, a person can, in a fundamental act of interpretation of his lifeworld that *uses* all of those elements but is not limited to them, forge *meaning* in his life.

In other words, a person can create a story of his life, a narrative of his existence, a framework of meaning, which draws upon all those other elements while at the same time providing the ethical context in which they operate and evolve. This meaning embodies a person's best knowledge and deepest intuitions about where he came from, what the real purpose of his being in this world is, and where (if anywhere at all) it might be leading after his last mortal breath. These constitute what the existentialist theologian Paul Tillich (1957) called a person's *ultimate concern*.

To the degree that a person is in touch with and acting from the ultimate concern(s) at the core of his existence, his life is charged with the indomita-ble energy of meaning. *Without* meaning, no set of circumstances, however pleasant, can ultimately sustain or satisfy a human being. *With* meaning, no set of circumstances, however difficult, can ultimately defeat an individual, who can find purpose, even joy, in the midst of his pain. Indeed, the pain may be the necessary catalyst that stimulated the unfolding into meaning.

In *Man's Search for Meaning*, Viktor Frankl (1967), a Jewish psychiatrist who survived the Nazi concentration camps, discussed how many individuals found meaning in their lives—even a connection with God—in the midst of their horrors. Conversely, the pampered trophy-wife driving a Mercedes Benz around Rodeo Drive in Beverly Hills, buying luxurious ornaments and gorgeous clothing, and getting cosmetic surgery every time she notices a wrinkle marring her Barbie-Doll "perfection" can—and often does—lead a life of despair born of meaninglessness.

Sometimes drugs can dull the existential pain of the vacuity of her life, but that brief escape only lasts until the next fix. Without meaning, any set of circumstances ultimately becomes an existential trap—a void and prison. With meaning, any set of circumstances, however painful, becomes the ground from which the individual can create an ever richer narrative of his life.

In fact, in psychotherapy the task is often not so much to change one's external conditions as to change one's understanding of them—to discover how they may fit together to deepen one's view of one's existence and to create a constructive trajectory toward a significant future (White & Epston, 1990). This narrative, which makes sense of the circumstances and points beyond them, thus helps one transcend those circumstances.

By *transcendence*, we are not necessarily referring to something beyond this world. The individual may find his ultimate meaning *in* this world, and this world alone—just as another may find it in the last analysis in something beyond this world. But in either case, the meaning that the person discovers in his life is *transcendent* because it is the "bird's-eye view" *above* the specific circumstances of his life that gives meaning *to* his life. *Education that helps teachers and students further their life-narratives is education for meaning, and it is the only form of education that is existentially vital and valid.*

It is this view of education for existential significance that we will explore in this chapter. Because we are drawing upon some basic ideas in existentialist philosophy, it is necessary to discuss a few of the most important ideas from that school of philosophy, which dominated the twentieth century and continue to exert a significant sway in this century.[1]

BASIC IDEAS IN EXISTENTIALIST PHILOSOPHY

The central idea in existentialist philosophy and psychology is that the most important thing that a person can do in life is to discover what is most important to him at the deepest level—and then to honor, explore, and extend that commitment or set of commitments as best he can in his unique *life-world*. To do this comprises what existentialism calls one's *life-project*. To pursue it courageously is what existentialism calls *living in good faith*—and this, according to existentialist ethics, is the height of ethical living..

Living in bad faith, on the other hand, resides in either not trying to discover what is most meaningful to oneself in one's life—or (even worse) knowing it but not living in it or up to it. It is a false life and thus the breeding ground of emotional despair, intellectual dishonesty, interpersonal phoniness, and political servitude.

According to existentialism, when an individual is living authentically in the light of his own self-discovered, self-defined, and therefore best and deepest meanings, he is a *being-for-himself* (Camus, 1970; Sartre, 1956).

This does not necessarily amount to raw selfishness, and usually not to selfishness at all. It simply means that one is living true to oneself, one's deepest intuitions about oneself, and, in that sense, *for* oneself. When a person tries to live according to someone else's program or image of what he should be, and not on the basis of his best ethical sense about the meaning(s) of his life, then that person no longer lives for himself. He lives *for* others. This is called *being-for-others* in existentialist philosophy.

Being-for-others has nothing to do with altruism or a sense of service to others. Indeed, a person who is being-for-others may be a crass materialist ever in search of more money and possessions. Such a person is not really *being-for-himself* if he is living in this way simply because he is just mind-lessly conforming to a soulless norm in a materialistic society such as ours.

After many years of absorbing wave after wave of explicit and implicit messages in the media that the faster the car, the bigger the house, and the easier the sex, the better; and after many years of subtle messages in schools and universities that what matters most is scoring high on standardized tests and landing a lucrative job—after all of this, the individual is not really living true to himself, not being-for-*himself*, but is aping a degraded and degrading social norm. He is conforming to the crowd, being-for-*others*.

Conversely, someone who has devoted his energy and resources in the service of others because it corresponds to his highest vision of things has realized the goal of *being-for-himself* in committing to and acting upon his most authentically and intensely felt convictions.

Existentialist psychotherapy sees *being-for-others* as the root of neurosis (May & Yalom, 1995). When we are untrue to who we are as individuals, the result is feelings of guilt (for having betrayed ourselves), panic (which always stems from losing touch with one's own being—a form of death), and disorientation (because one's life is no longer guided by the true North Star of self-awareness). To be for others means that one has become "objectified"—an object of someone else's purposes or program.

The same is true at the political level. In a consumer society, individuals tend to lose their status *as* individuals (or *subjects*) and become *objects*—to be economically and politically manipulated, largely through statistical analysis, electronic surveillance, and, indeed, by the whole apparatus of corporate control that we now increasingly find ourselves (and our schools) caught in. In such a consumer society, perversely powered by the pathology of what Marx called "commodity fetishism," the person falls out of living relationship with himself and, consequently, with other people and with his work.

This is what Marx called *alienation*—from self, others, and labor. It is another term for living in bad faith. When the agencies that exercise power over individuals are able to convince them that this is the way things should be, thus seducing them to give more and more of themselves over to the corporate complex of control, then those individuals are said to be living in *false consciousness.*

Education that seduces children—with the bait of grades, status, and possessions—into uncritical conformity is education for false consciousness. And this is too often the state of things in our schools today.

By means of increasing standardization (as imposed on schools by the new corporate masters) our educational sites are turning into places where teachers and students are whipped into uniformity through the lavish rewards and humiliating punishments of not scoring well on standardized tests. They are thereby turned into objects, trained into false consciousness, alienated from themselves and others, and rewarded for losing the connection with their unique core selves.

This is education for neurosis—a pedagogy of psychosocial pathology—and it is having predictably tragic results on our children, many of whom are increasingly being diagnosed with all sorts of "behavioral" and "learning" disorders.

In a high percentage of these cases what we are really seeing is not evidence of children having "illnesses" but of them acting out against the illness of the classroom itself—the mind- and soul-numbing joylessness and anti-creativity of life in the standardized classroom today. And when the student's quite natural rejection of the sterility of the classroom becomes too pronounced, he is diagnosed with an "illness" and drugged into submission with pharmaceuticals provided by the same corporate system that caused the problem in the first place.

Being-for-oneself, on the other hand, is the source of creativity, realistic compassion, and emotional empowerment. Education that promotes *being for oneself* is what is truly needed if we wish to create a society filled with sane and powerful people who can make our nation both great and good. Our educational sites and processes should exist primarily in the service of psychosocial empowerment of students and teachers, for such empowerment is crucial to individual and communal wellbeing.

In 1988, the dean of American educational history, Lawrence Cremin, warned that the major specter that would haunt the United States in the twenty-first century would be the metastasizing of the cancerous military-industrial complex into the "military-industrial-*educational* complex." Our major challenge as educators, he predicted, would be to find ways to resist it. His prophecy has come to pass. As educators we must find ways to *educate for existential authenticity* in order to resist the incursion of the corporate behemoth into our educational spaces.

How a teacher fosters narratives of empowerment and hope in his students will often vary from class to class, even student to student. However, in what follows we will discuss some of the most crucial features of teaching for transcendence and transformation: 1) education as caring, 2) education as art, 3) education as liberation, 4) education as encounter, and 5) education as spirit.

KEY CONCEPTS IN EXISTENTIAL PEDAGOGY

Education as Caring: A Relational Pedagogy

In his famous hierarchy-of-needs pyramid, Maslow placed at the very top of the pyramid of needs what he considered to be the most important one of all—the desire to self-actualize. As a theorist and practitioner who was instrumental in the last half of the twentieth century in defining education as the enrichment of the student's existential lifeworld, Maslow's ideas are central in defining education for existential authenticity:

> If we want to be helpers, counselors, teachers, guides, or psychotherapists, what we must do is to accept the person and help him learn what kind of person he is already. What is his style, what are his aptitudes, what is the person good for, not good for, what can we build upon, what are his good raw materials, his potentialities?. . .Above all, we [should] care for the child, that is, enjoy him and his growth and his self-actualization. (1968, p. vi)

In the existentially sensitive curriculum, the student is offered ways for him to make sense of his own life-world (Greene, 1974). What he studies is grist for the mill as he interprets and carries on his life as truly to himself and as serviceably to others as he can.

Because this view of educational processes is so tightly focused on individual uniqueness, there are no one-size-fits-all pedagogical tools or methodologies that can create zones for self-actualization in the classroom. It is an attitude *toward* the student, not a program *for* him, which lies at the heart of existentially rich pedagogy. This attitude can best be described as *care*. Care means *reverence* for who the student is at his core, *gratitude* for the chance to help him expand his intellectual horizons, and *excitement* at seeing the student make an idea his own, and in his own way, and then fold it into his own life-story in order to vitalize his existence.

A pedagogy of deep caring—existential caring—is not coddling.[2] It is not the saccharine pedagogy of just making sure that students play "nice" and feel "good" about themselves at the end of the day because they were never particularly challenged to do anything difficult or to move out of their comfort zones. Rather, it sets the highest of all possible standards—that the student engage an activity or idea in the classroom as fully as he can, and always with an eye to enfolding what he has learned into his life-story so that he is truer to himself and more genuine with others.

When this happens, education goes beyond the mere training and memorizing that characterize standardized education—education as the mere *transmission* of facts and figures, education to turn the individual into an *object*. It becomes *transformation* of self, other and world—education to help a student in his ongoing project of becoming an ever deeper *subject* (Kane, 1999).

Education as Art: "Poetic" Knowing

This feature of existentially fruitful education has to do with the distinction in the preceding chapter between *mathetic* (analytical) and *poetic* (intuitive) knowing. In the existential domain, the premium is on poetic ways of knowing. This is the case whether the subject is clearly in the poetic domain, as in art, or clearly in the mathetic domain, as in physics.

What qualifies a subject as being handled poetically is that it is used primarily as a springboard for a student to explore and expand his existence, and to then express this experience in words, actions, and products that betoken his growth.

From making a cutting board in a woodshop class to experiencing the power of an image in a Shakespearian sonnet, from charting a chemical reaction in a lab to running the 100-meter hurdles, virtually any idea or activity at a school can be an occasion for a student to grasp his existence more vitally, intuit its possible directions more subtly, and act on all of this more lucidly. Global, intuitive, and idiosyncratic, this way of knowing is deeply poetic. It is in this sense that

> any activity—indeed, at their very best, activities that are engaged in to court surprise, to cultivate discovery, to find new forms of experience—is expressive in character. Nothing in the sciences, the home or mechanical arts, or in social relationships prohibits or diminishes the possibility of engaging in expressive outcomes. (Huebner, 1999, p. 393)

Because this way of educating revolves around the uses of intuition and expression in the service of the care and cultivation of the individual, it is often called "humanist-aesthetic" (Ornstein & Hunkins, 1988). Such pedagogies are also "aesthetic" because the goal is for the student to experience any topic or activity in the classroom as one would experience a work of art. What does it mean for a student to experience a subject as a critic would a piece of art? Well, consider what happens when an art critic views a painting.

In looking at the painting, the idea is to approach the piece with as finely focused concentration as is possible. Not taking anything for granted, he is always trying to see the piece with as much freshness of mind and clarity of judgment as is possible. This means always being open to surprising new visions of what the painting is and what it suggests.

When this happens, the painting reveals endless layers and types of meaning from viewing to viewing. The painting is not a static product. It is a living process—dynamic, open-ended, and varying from viewer to viewer. And of course, the confrontation with the piece of art becomes *meaningful* only when it casts light on the viewer's own existence—that existence's present state, its limitations and possibilities, its strengths and shortcomings, and, above all, its trajectory towards an ever more meaningful future.

When teachers and students engage a subject poetically—mining it for its existential gold—then the curriculum is being experienced in an aesthetic manner. The curriculum becomes a living organism, not a dead object. And as both teacher and student enter into dialogue with each other through dialogue with the living curriculum, they, too, become more alive. Thus as the existentialist curriculum theorist Max van Manen has wisely observed:

> It is probably less correct to say that we learn *about* the subjects contained in the school curriculum than that the subjects let us know something. It is in this letting us know that subject matter becomes a true subject: a subject which makes relationship possible. The subject calls upon us in such a way that its otherness, its it-ness, turns into the dialogic Other: the "you." In this way our responsiveness, our "listening" to the subject, constitutes the very essence of the relationship of a student with subject matter. (1990, p. 31)

The philosopher of art Theodore Meyer Greene said that "a work of art is a unique, individual whole—a self-contained artistic 'organism' with a 'life' and 'reality' of its own. . . . The competent critic. . . apprehends the individual work of art in all its self-contained uniqueness through sensitive artistic recreation" (Greene, 1953, p. 414). Similarly, the teacher must help the student "recreate" a subject (which, no less than a work of art, is also "a self-contained . . . 'organism' with a 'life' and 'reality' of its own") so that the student experientially makes it his own.

To accomplish this, the teacher must move the student—sometimes tenderly, sometimes forcefully—beyond the easy, standard interpretations of the subject matter in order to confront the issues under discussion with the same intensity, curiosity, and creativity as in confronting a piece of art for the first time. The teacher, no less than the student, must come face-to-face with the subject matter in true encounter—and this means with the emotional clarity and moral courage that a good critic brings to his face-to-face with a work of art.

Education as Liberation: "Conscientizacion"

The existential curriculum rests on the idea that we are existentially obliged to construct ourselves not only individually but also collectively in ever greater degrees of humane and responsible freedom. Democracy is a political expression of the existential ideal of free individuals in mutually respectful, mutually enriching dialogue in the wider setting of a civic body. Perhaps the most important 20th-century educational prophet of this dual existential vision of personal and political freedom was the educational theorist Paolo Freire. He wrote:

> Insofar as I am a conscious presence in the world, I cannot hope to escape my responsibility for my action in the world. . . . At the heart of the experience of coherently democratic authority is a basic, almost obsessive dream: namely, to persuade or convince freedom of its vocation to autonomy as it travels the road of self-construction, using materials from within and without, but elaborated over and over again. It is within this autonomy, laboriously constructed, that freedom will gradually occupy those spaces previously inhabited by dependency. (2001, pp. 26, 87)

This is Freire's well-known pedagogical practice of *conscientizacion*, roughly translated as "becoming aware." It means teaching for consciousness-raising, both one's own and one's students'. *Conscientizacion* views the curriculum as an instrument of liberation in the classroom in the service of liberation of oneself and others in the larger world outside the classroom.

Freire began his teaching and theorizing among the very poor in order to help them find personally meaningful ways to define and deal with their socioeconomic oppression (Freire, 1970). As his theorizing evolved, he began to view oppression more broadly as any set of internal or external constraints that hinder an individual—regardless of his socioeconomic status—from being able to take hold of his existence and build it up in ways that manifest his best ethical intuitions and talents (Freire, 1970).

Education as *conscientizacion* sees the curriculum as a tool that the student can use to examine his life, expose those forces that are illegitimately constricting it, and devise ways of unfettering it so as to live a life of greater scope, wisdom, and compassion.

The chains that the student wishes to shake off may be primarily political or economic ones. However, these are not the only chains that bind.

A boy who is discovering himself as a ballet dancer in a dance class and is thus breaking free of his father's brutish notions of masculinity is engaging in education as liberation. A girl who, in studying images of women in literature from other cultures, is learning how to reject the demeaning images of womanhood purveyed by American advertising, is also involved in education as liberation. And the teacher who is aiding his students in these ways is himself becoming freer and more empowered in rising to his full professional stature as a guide to his students—an exemplar of how freedom is found, manifested, and exercised in intelligent goodness. Such a teacher, by his very presence, generates hope in his students, who now experience

> trust in the world because this [teacher] exists. That is the most inward achievement of the relation in education. Because this human being exists, meaninglessness, no matter how hard pressed you are by it, cannot be the real truth. Because this human being exists, in the darkness the light lies hidden, in fear salvation, and in the callousness of one's fellow-men the great Love. (Buber, 1985, p. 98)

Education as Encounter: The "I-Thou" Classroom

All talk of existentially responsive education amounts to nothing if a student is not seen and treated respectfully in the classroom. A student cannot be treated like an anonymous object and be expected to develop as a responsible subject. The degree to which a teacher may engage each student individually will vary, of course, depending upon institutional guidelines, class size, resources, and the student's own willingness to do so.

But at any educational site that claims existential authenticity, there must be a basic attitude of what one might call *existential regard* for the student as a unique being, and this attitude must prevail in how teachers and students interact with each other. Where a student is treated as an object, no curriculum, however rich in existential potential, can really be existentially fruitful because, even though the teacher may talk the talk of helping students develop deeply, he is not walking the walk of authentic encounter with them.

Crucial to existentially fertile education is an *I-Thou* relationship between the teacher and student, not *I-It*. According to the Jewish existentialist theologian Martin Buber, an *I-Thou* relationship occurs in dialogue when individuals are intellectually sincere with and emotionally attuned to each other. The relationship, one of *care-full* listening and speaking, promotes each person's existential journey.

An *I-It* relationship, on the other hand, is deeply unethical, for in such a relationship one person is trying to turn the other into an object, an "it," a mere instrument to serve his plans or programs with no regard for the other's individual nature or needs (Buber, 1965).

An *I-It* relationship is destructive because the "I" in this dyad has no interest in exploring or empowering the other person as a unique "Thou" with great existential potential. Instead, the "I" of the *I-it* relationship, seeing the other person as an object of its own domineering desires and acquisitive goals, tries to negate the other's existential identity in order to feed its own insatiable appetite and will. Yet, because we attain existential authenticity in ourselves only to the degree that we respond to it in others, we close the door on our own existential growth whenever we "objectify" another person in any fashion.

Buber saw *I-Thou* relationship as both the origin and goal of any deeply educational situation, for ideally "the relation in education is one of pure dialogue." The *I-Thou* relationship being the cornerstone of morality, he made what he called "dialogical ethics" the foundation of his pedagogy.

In dialogical pedagogy, the relationship between the teacher and student is the nucleus around which everything else spins. The curriculum is the occasion for this relationship to happen. As a theologian, Buber even went so far as to claim that when a teacher and student are engaged in rich relationship, they reach not only intellectual but truly spiritual heights, coming into contact with Divinity, "the eternal *Thou*." "The extended lines of relation meet in the eternal *Thou*," wrote Buber in his classic work *I and Thou*, and

> every particular *Thou* is a glimpse through to the eternal *Thou*; by means of every particular *Thou*, the primary word addresses the eternal *Thou*. Through the mediation of the *Thou* of all beings, fulfillment, and non-fulfillment, of relations comes to them: The inborn *Thou* is realized in each relation and consummated in none. (Buber, 1965, p. 75).

On the other hand, in an *I-It* pedagogy the teacher and student soon find themselves in an interpersonal and spiritual wasteland, for "if a man lets it have the mastery, the continuing growing world of *It* overruns him and robs him of the reality of his own *I*, till the incubus over him and the ghost within him whisper to one another the confession of their non-salvation" (Buber, 1965, p. 46).

Thus it is imperative that the existentially authentic teacher enter into a relationship with the student in increasingly deep encounter. The subject under analysis in the classroom is not a thing unto itself but rather the curricular infrastructure of this essentially ethical process of relationship in education. This is a process that *rests upon* subject matter but ultimately *transcends* it as the teacher and student, through dialogical encounter, approach the realm of meaning in their individual lifeworlds.

Whatever sets itself up against relationship in education—and this is, of course, precisely what standardized forms of instruction and assessment by definition do—commits moral violence. It is also intellectually inadequate because the teacher and student will achieve the most profound forms of understanding of the subject matter by exploring it together.

In the *I-Thou* classroom, discourse must be honest, whether that honesty be comfortable or not to the members of a classroom; for, what is dishonest could hardly be considered ethical. To be sure, *I-Thou* conversation must always be civil.

Uncivil discourse—such as abounds on radio and television talk shows, in which the object is not really to make a useful point but to skewer and even humiliate an opponent—never results in any ultimate good. How could it? Existentially authentic discourse is mindful of the ethical up-building of oneself and others through (inter)penetrating encounter, not the public shaming of others through merely slick verbal attacks. *I-Thou* discourse *must* be civil.

However, it need not always be *comfortable*. Indeed, existentially authentic conversation will sometimes *not* be comfortable because each conversant may be being challenged to examine and even change deeply held convictions.

Dishonest discourse designed to keep things superficially "friendly" in the classroom by timidly evading real differences in points-of-view and conclusions among the participants is (be it ever so "polite") not authentic. Not being authentic, it is not constructive. Not being constructive, it is not truly *care-full* of oneself and others. It is, therefore, although sweet-seeming, not really *I-Thou* discourse but simply a polite version of unethical *I-It* talk.

Civil, frank, and characterized by genuine listening to others and humility in speaking one's own truth, *I-Thou* classroom discourse is both open and humane. It is an approach to conversation in which the conversant is like the character in Chaucer's *Canterbury Tales* of whom it was said, "Gladly would he learn, and gladly teach."

Healthy humor—not demeaning to anyone or any group of people in any way—can play a significant role in the creation of an *I-Thou* classroom. Laughter can humanize things, tempering the high drama of existentially authentic encounter with a well-timed chuckle. Just as the comic-relief scenes in *Hamlet, King Lear,* or *Julius Caesar* give the audience a chance to breathe, relax, and reconstitute themselves for the next crucial existential moment, so a good laugh in the classroom can be restorative, bonding, and clarifying.

Furthermore, a teacher must always be resisting the temptation to engage in "power talk" if he wishes to foster real communication. Power talk is any talk that is meant to illegitimately assert the teacher's inherent power in the classroom in order to shut a student down. There are many varieties of power talk. Often it consists of the teacher trying to run circles around students by whipping out obscure, unnecessarily technical, and arrogant language.

For the student, such talk is disempowering and demeaning. Power talk is a sort of verbal web that a teacher maliciously spins in order to immobilize and then devour the student psychologically, politically, and morally.

Power talk is also a steamroller that the teacher mounts in order to force his interpretation of something onto students who have not had the chance to explore it in such a way as to *feel* their ways through it individually, poke inquisitively into its various corners and alleys, peaks and valleys, and thereby make it their own in their own way and for their own purposes. This is the only kind of classroom discourse that produces free individuals in *I-Thou* conversation. Indeed, "the natural educative consequences of conversation are broken when the power relations between speaker and listener are unequal and when power is used [by the teacher] to impose an interpretation" (Huebner, 1999, p. 256).

Simply put, power talk in the classroom is unethical. "The teacher who does not respect the student's curiosity in its diverse aesthetic, linguistic, and syntactic expressions; who uses irony to put down legitimate questioning. . .; who is not respectfully present in the educational experience of the student, transgresses fundamental ethical principles of the human condition (Freire, 2001, p. 59).

And besides being wrong, power talk is pedagogically *useless* because no one will truly accept an imposed interpretation, however much he may slavishly feign agreement in the classroom in order to appease the teacher—and then, most likely, mock the teacher as soon as he is out of the teacher's sight.

Not power talk but *em*powering talk should be the gold-standard in the existentially rich classroom.

Education as Spirituality: The Sacred Space of the Classroom

For some teachers and students, educational processes and products attain their greatest significance only when they point beyond themselves to a realm of spirit that transcends this world in every way—while investing itself in this world at every turn.

For such individuals, education must ultimately revolve around this Spirit in order for education to have existential validity. For, inviting, invoking, being with, and celebrating this Presence *is* their ultimate concern. For them, education is one of the primary vehicles that the individual rides in his ongoing trajectory towards communion with and celebration of the Absolute Other, the Divine, which, although invisible and often enough incomprehensible to us, gives visible life and meaning to everything we see. Since it is in the light of this Spirit that such individuals ultimately inhabit and interpret their lifeworlds, education that exists in and for the Spirit as it dwells uniquely in each of them is of maximum existential worth to them.

Education in the spirit is not typically "religious," nor need it even be obviously "spiritual." The only requirement is that it be an occasion for the individual—in his own quiet and particular way—to seek out the presence of the Divine that inheres in educational processes and products. This can happen on a football field, in an art class, within a lab, in a discussion about literature, or on a theatrical stage.

As perhaps the greatest of all curricular theorists, Duane Huebner, has declared, any educational content or relationship may be a dwelling place for the Divine. The Spirit, Huebner asserts, is inevitably present in existentially authentic education. "Hovering always is the absolute 'other,' Spirit, that overwhelms us in moments of awe, terror, tragedy, beauty, and peace. Content is the 'other.' Knowing is the process of being in relationship with that 'other.' Knowledge is an abstraction from that process." To define the goal of education in lesser terms is a mistake, for "the journey of the self is short circuited or derailed by those who define the ends of life and education in less than ultimate terms."[3]

Huebner notes in similar strains that "the otherness that informs and accompanies education is the absolute Otherness, the transcendent Other, however we name that which goes beyond appearances and all conditions. Education is the lure of the transcendent—that openness to a future that is beyond all futures" (Huebner, 1999, p. 360). When teaching and learning occur under the pull of that lure, when it is a trajectory toward the transcendent, education occurs in and for the Spirit.

The Divine may announce itself in the classroom all of a sudden to everyone present. This is what happens in the story told by Martin Buber in his essay "On Teaching." Here he portrays a young teacher entering a classroom full of unruly boys at the beginning of a term in geography. Understandably defensive, the teacher's initial impulse is to assert his power in order to establish control—and just

> to say No, to say No to everything rising against him from beneath. . . . And if one starts from beneath one perhaps never arrives above, but everything comes down. But then his eyes meet a face which strikes him. It is not a beautiful face nor particularly intelligent; but it is a real face, or rather, the chaos preceding the cosmos of a real face. On it he reads a question which is something different from the general curiosity. . . . And he, the young teacher, addresses this face. He says nothing very ponderous or important, he puts an ordinary introductory question: "What did you talk about last in geography? The Dead Sea? Well, what about the Dead Sea?" But there was obviously something not quite usual in the question, for the answer he gets is not the ordinary schoolboy answer; the boy begins to *tell a story*. Some months earlier he had stayed for a few hours on the shores of the Dead Sea and it is of this he tells. He adds: "And everything looked to me as if it had been created a day before the rest of creation." Quite unmistakably he had only in this moment made up his mind to talk about it. In the meantime his face has changed. It is no longer quite as chaotic as before. And the class has fallen silent. They all listen. The class, too, is no longer a chaos. Something has happened. The young teacher has started from above. (Buber, 1985, pp. 112-113)

Although such moments as these are not rare in the existentially vibrant classroom, neither are they the norm. More typically, the Spirit addresses the *individual* student and teacher in the classroom in silent, idiosyncratic, quite unpredictable ways throughout the day, alerting him that what he is experiencing in the classroom can be absorbed into the larger narrative of his life, holding out to him the promise of greater involvement in his own depths, where the Divine stirs him, meets him, and, in showing him how to be more like himself, makes him more like Itself.

In the existentially vital curriculum, the student and teacher increasingly learn to attend to the Zen imperative: "Become who you are!"

APPLICATIONS: THE EXISTENTIAL DIMENSION

Coming to an authentic understanding of themselves is an important quest for students to undertake; through this process, students gain insight into what they believe, value, and intuit in themselves. This life task takes the form of truth seeking, which prepares students to live life in *good faith*. Living life in good faith is the ability to explore and discover one's real purpose for being in this world, and to live life true to the commitments, values, and quests that follow. The existentialist curriculum dimension helps students develop greater clarity about themselves and find learning more pleasurable and meaningful.

Teachers can weave existential learning experiences into the content areas of history, literature, or science, or through themes such as conflict and adversity that cut across the curriculum.

HISTORY

As part of a study of the westward expansion in U.S. history, teachers could lead students through a dialogue that runs as a strand throughout the whole study and is continuously charted on posters that are kept on display in the classroom. To inform this continuing dialogue, students could be asked to keep track of the following in their journals from their content readings.

- Movement into the unknown
- Encountering obstacles to their forward movement: mountains, huge rivers, wildernesses
- Physical travails: hunger, cold, heat, injuries
- Dangerous animals: snakes, cougars, wolves,
- Psychological tests:
- And so forth….
  Sample of List that Could Be Kept on Poster

Box 5.1

1. List the challenges the men and women who participated in the westward movement likely encountered. Be prepared to discuss them in a small group.
2. Chart the characteristics men and women who successful confronted these challenges would likely possess. Show evidence for each characteristic from what you've read.
3. Relate what you've read about the Westward Movement to your own lives through a written reflection. Follow the directions below:

    a. Describe the six characteristics that you admired most in individuals who played an important role in the westward movement.

    — Explain why you think these characteristics are important.

    — Which of these characteristics do you see in yourself? What evidence do you see? How do these characteristics help you achieve your life's purposes?

    — Which of these characteristics would you like to develop? How might you go about developing these characteristics? If you are successful, how might these characteristics contribute to you achieving your life's purposes?

SCIENCE, LITERATURE, AND HISTORY

Society has benefited from many extraordinary individuals who have brought new knowledge into the world and provided leadership to the nations and

Table 5.1

Characteristic	Evidence from Study of Westward Expansion (text, articles, biographies, etc.)
Courageous	_____
Adventurous	_____
Naïve	_____
Determined	_____
Hard-working	_____
Desperate	_____
Visionary	_____
Independent	_____
Individualistic	_____
Creative	_____
Intelligent	_____
Cautious	_____
And so forth . . .	_____

countries of the world during crises. Examples of these individuals from science are Marie Curie, Louis Pasteur, the Wright Brothers, and Leonardo da Vinci. Individuals from history could be Nelson Mandela, Winston Churchill, Harry Truman, Louis and Clark, George Washington, and Thomas Jefferson.

Students can gain an understanding of these exemplary individuals, as well as develop insight into themselves by studying biographies or expository accounts of these men and women. Following is an essay assignment that could stimulate students to process new knowledge through the existential dimension.

MAKING CONNECTIONS TO SELF

1. Describe the types of courage that these extraordinary individuals would likely have possessed in order to achieve what they did in their lives?
2. Which types of courage do you think were most significant in what this/these individual(s) achieved in their lives?
3. Which types of courage do you see in yourself? Under what circumstances have you had to use that courage?
4. Which of these types of courage would you like to develop? How might you go about cultivating that type of courage in yourself? In others?
5. Based on what you observed in this/these individual(s), how might you define courage for yourself? How will you use this definition as a guide to help yourself move forward?

CONFLICT AND ADVERSITY: CROSS-CUTTING THEMES FOR ALL CONTENT AREAS

Every person deals with conflict and encounters adversity in their lives. By examining content through these two lenses, students will make connections between and within content areas and explore and expand self-knowledge in the process. Following are some learning experiences that teachers could use to engage students in this process.

Conflict. Student could examine multiple situations in which conflict was a prominent factor. These situations could be drawn from current events, history, the world of science, or literature. From this study, students could create an individual and collective definition of conflict through self-reflection and dialogue. Once that definition is developed, students could do the following:

1. Analyze conditions that seem to contribute to conflict.
2. List examples of conflict.
3. Determine how conflict contributes to or detracts from society at large:
   a. Citizens of the world?
   b. Citizens of our country?
   c. Neighbors?
   d. Friends?
   e. Me?
4. Identify factors that must be present in the resolution of conflict. How might one become an active contributor to the resolution of conflict with:
   a. Classmates at school?
   b. Family members?
   c. Friends?
5. What types of conflicts might one feel within him- or herself?
   a. In what ways is it healthy?
   b. In what ways is it problematic?
   c. What skills do I have to cope with conflict in my life?

Adversity. Individuals through the ages have encountered adversity. Some are famous, such as Anne Frank or Victor Frankel, while others are ordinary citizens, such as the authors of this book. Sometimes whole cultures encounter adversity like the pogroms perpetrated against the Jewish people during World War II and the abuse suffered by African slaves in early American history. By studying the adversity others have encountered and then relating it to their own life story, students could gain insights and develop personal coping skills for when they encounter adversity. Following is a way teachers could have students examine adversity:

1. Study individuals or a people who have encountered adversity.
   a. Describe the adversities they encountered.
   b. Examine the dispositions and skills they possessed that helped them cope with their adversities.
2. What might you do if you encountered that same adversity?
3. Identify the skills and dispositions that would help you cope with adversity.
4. Explain how understanding the way these individuals or people coped with their adversity could help you manage yours.

Chapter Five

NOTES

1. We have drawn especially the work of Jean Paul Sartre (1956), Martin Heidegger (1964), and Albert Camus (1970). Also important in forming the ideological foundation of this chapter has been the work of the religious Existentialist writers Soren Kierkegaard (1969), Martin Buber (1965), and Paul Tillich (1957).

2. Nel Noddings' term for this is "ontological caring."

3. Standardized "education" is the most obvious culprit, of course, in this "short circuiting" and "derailing" of the individual's trek down the many paths of education toward the god within.

Conclusion

The Humane Teacher

When teaching and learning occur in a way that addresses the major dimensions of human experience—organic, psychodynamic, affiliative, procedural, and existential—they speak to the whole person. This is why holistic education is the most humane education.

For in attending to the whole person, education fulfills its ultimate purpose, which must clearly be to promote health, creativity, purpose, and growth. When educational agendas focus on only one aspect of the student, the other aspects of the person must atrophy and die, and the resulting toxicity then seeps throughout the individual's total system and infects it. Physical, emotional, cultural, intellectual, and ethical diseases result.

To be sure, education may legitimately stress or even exclusively focus upon one of the facets of the student as a total being. But it must do so for specific purposes and in limited doses only. If education is in one domain only (usually the cognitive domain in the contemporary American classroom) which then becomes the only fare for the student to the exclusion of other educational nourishment, then the student becomes "holistically malnourished," even "starved," just as a person develops all sorts of illnesses if there is no variation and balance in his or her diet. Indeed, education that is carried on in one domain only is not education at all, really. It is "training."

Training in specific domains for specific purposes certainly has its place. However, training should never be confused with education and made the "agenda" for a nation's entire educational system. If it is, the results are disastrous to not only the student but the teacher. *Education* means that the whole individual, *as* an individual, is being offered ideas, materials, activities, encounters, and experiences that promote his or her growth as a human being, in rich association with other human beings, and all in the service of making meaning of his or her life, and of what might lie beyond this life.

125

When this happens, education is an ethical endeavor. However, as the study of the history of American education shows beyond any possibility of controversy, when corporate agencies constrict the scope of education to just one domain, it is invariably in order to commandeer education, to turn schools into instruments by which the corporate masters of our societies seek to impose a political or economic agenda on teachers and students—and, ultimately, on an entire people.

Hence, when schools are not places where the whole child is being nurtured, this should be understood as much more than just a "school issue." There is good reason for all citizens to fear that larger forces are at work in the political economy when the agendas imposed on schools aim at transforming teachers and students into cogs in the new corporate machine. When this happens, it is not only students and teachers who are being targeted but, ultimately, everyone.

As the Progressive pedagogues of the early twentieth century realized, humane education and a vibrant democracy go hand in hand. The very title of the most significant educational text of the twentieth century written in 1916 by the most important educational theorist of that century—*Democracy and Education* by John Dewey—suggests that the complete nurturance of the student throughout his or her education is an indispensable prerequisite of a viable democracy.

As Dewey argued, when individuals are not whole—not moving individually and collectively in organically, psychosocially, intellectually, and existentially healthy directions—they become fragmented, alienated, cynical, bored, and therefore *manipulable*. They are then the easy prey of any passing fad or sly demagogue—especially those fads and demagogues that camouflage themselves in the rhetoric of democracy but are really ravening wolves of the corporate order, hell-bent on subjugating, even obliterating, the individual in all of his or her glorious uniqueness and eternal potential.

Teaching is the noblest of all the professions. It is an art second to none. It it is to help teachers practice that profession and art as humanely as possible—and thus resist those darker forces that would turn education into something less than the high endeavor that it ultimately is—that we have written this book. If it has been successful in even a small measure in accomplishing this goal, the authors will be well pleased.

Bibliography

Adams, D. (1995). *Education for extinction: American Indians and the boarding school experience, 1875–1928*. Lawrence: University Press of Kansas.

Adler, A. (1930). *The education of children*. Tr. E. Jensen and F. Jensen. South Bend, IN: George Allen and Unwin, Ltd.

Almon, J. (1999). "From Cognitive Learning to Creative Thinking," in *Education, Information, and Transformation: Essays on Learning and Thinking*, Ed. J. Kane Columbus, OH: Merrill, 1999, 254.

Arredondo, P., Toporek, R., Brown, S. P., Jones, J., Locke, D. C., Sanchez, J., and Stadler, H. (1996). Operationalization of multicultural counseling competencies. *Journal of Multicultural Counseling and Development*, 24, 42–78.

Au, K., and Kawakami, A. (1985). Research currents: Talk story and learning to read. *Language Arts*, 62(4), 406–11.

Ballantine, J. (1997). *The sociology of education: A systematic analysis*. Upper Saddle River, NJ: Prentice Hall.

Belenky, M., Clinchy, B., Goldberger, N., and Tarule, J. (1986). *Women's way of knowing*. New York: Basic Books.

Black, P., Wiliam, D. (2001). Inside the black box: Raising standards through classroom assessment. In D. Wiliam (Ed.), London: Kings College London School of Education.

Brophy, J. (1994). *Motivating students to learn*. Boston: McGraw-Hill.

Broudy, H., and Palmer, J. (1965). *Exemplars of teaching method*. Chicago: Rand McNally and Company.

Brown, J., Collins, A., and Duguid, O. (1988). Situated cognition and the culture of learning. *Educational Researcher*, 18: pp. 32-42.

Bruner, J. (1996). *The culture of education*. Cambridge, MA: Harvard University Press.

Buber, M. (1985). *Between man and man*. New York: Scribners.

———. (1965). *I and thou*. New York: Vintage.

Bullough, R. (2001). *Uncertain lives: Children of hope, teachers of promise*. New York: Teachers College, Columbia University.

Camus, A. (1970). *Lyrical and critical essays*. New York: Vintage.

Celsi, T. (1990). *The fourth little pig*. Milwaukee: Raintree Publishers.

Chi, M. T. H., Feltovich, P. J., Glaser, R. (1981). Categorization and representation of physics problems by experts and novices. *Cognitive Science*. 5, pp. 121–52.

Collier, V. (1995). Acquiring a second language [Electronic Version]. *Directions in Language and Education*, 1. Retrieved April 11, 2006, from http://www.ncela.gwu.edu/pubs/directions/04.htm .

Conger, J., and Galambos, J. (1997). *Adolescence and youth: Psychological development in a changing world.* New York: Longman.

Counts, G. (1932). *Dare the school build a new social order?* New York: John Day.

Crain, W. (1992). *Theories of development: Concepts and applications.* Englewood Cliffs, NJ: Prentice-Hall.

Cremin, L. (1964). *The transformation of the school: Progressivism in American education, 1876–1957.* New York: Vintage Press.

———. (1988). *American education: The metropolitan experience:* New York: Harper and Row.

Cummins, J. (2000). *Language, power, and pedagogy: Bilingual children in the crossfire.* Buffalo, NY: Multilingual Matters.

Devine, D. (1995). Prejudice and out-group perception. In A. Tesser (Ed.). *Advanced social psychology* (pp. 467-524). New York: McGraw-Hill.

Dewey, J. (1904). in G. Willis, W. Schubert, R. Bullough, Jr., C. Kridel and J. Holton. *The American Curriculum: A Documentary History* London: Praeger, 1994, 126.

Eisner, E., and Vallance, E. (1985). *The educational imagination: On the design and evaluation of school programs.* New York: Macmillan.

Eliade, M. (1974). *The myth of the eternal return or, Cosmos and history.* Princeton, NJ: Princeton University Press.

Elkind, D. (1968). Cognitive development in adolescence. In J. Adams (Ed.). *Understanding adolescence* (pp. 128–58). Boston: Allyn and Bacon.

Ellenberger, Henri F. (1970). *The discovery of the unconscious: The history and evolution of dynamic psychiatry.* New York: Basic Books.

Erickson, F. (2001). Culture in society and in educational practices. In J. Banks and C. Banks (Eds.), *Multicultural Education: Issues and Perspectives* (4th edition). pp. 31–58. New York: Wiley.

Fay, B. (1987). *Critical Social Science: Liberation and its Limits.* Ithaca, NY: Cornell University Press.

———. (2000). *Contemporary philosophy of social science: A multicultural approach.* Oxford: Blackwell Publishers Ltd.

Ferdman, B. M. (1990). Literacy and Cultural Identity. *Harvard Educational Review*, 60(2), 181–204.

Ferrer, J. (2002). *Revisioning transpersonal theory: A participatory vision of human spirituality.* Albany: State University of New York Press.

Forlini, G., Williams, E. J., & Brinkman, A. (2010). *Class acts: Every teacher's guide to activate learning.* Bronxville, NY: Lavender Hills.

Foucault, M. (1979). *Discipline and punish.* New York: Vintage Books.

Freire, P. (2001). *Pedagogy and freedom: Ethics, democracy, and civic courage.* New York: Rowman & Littlefield, 2001.

———. (1970). *The pedagogy of the oppressed.* New York: Seabury Press.

Frankl, V. (1967) *Man's search for meaning.* New York: Washington Square Press.

Gass, S. M., and Selinker, L. (1994). *Second language acquisition: An introductory course.* Hillsdale, NJ: Lawrence Erlbaum Associates, Publishers.

Gauvain, M. (2001). *The social context of cognitive development* (Vol. 4). New York: Guilford Press.

Gay, G. (2000). *Culturally responsive teaching: Theory, research and practice.* New York: Teacher College Press.

Gibson, M. (1988). *Accommodation without assimilation: Sikh immigrants in an American high school.* Ithaca, NY: Cornell University Press.

Giddens, A. (1990). *The consequences of modernity.* Stanford: Stanford University Press.

———. (1991). *Modernity and self-identity: Self and society in the late modern age.* Stanford: Stanford University Press.

Gilligan, C. (1982). *In a different voice: Psychological theory and women's development.* Cambridge, MA: Harvard University Press.

Goffman, E. (1997). *The Goffman reader.* C. Lemert, and A. Branaman (Eds.). London: Blackwell.

Greene, M. (1974). Cognition, consciousness, and curriculum. In W. Pinar (Ed). *Heightened consciousness, cultural revolution, and curriculum theory* (pp. 69–83). Berkeley, CA: McCutchan Publishing.

Greene, T. "The Function of Criticism." In *The Problems of Aesthetics,* eds. E. Vivas and M. Krieger. New York: Reinhart (1953): 414–18.

Greenspan, S. (1989). Emotional intelligence. In K. Field, B. Cohler, and G. Wool (eds), *Learning and Education: Psychoanalytic Perspectives* Madison, CT: International Universities Press, Inc., 209–44.

Grossman, H. (1995). *Teaching in a diverse society.* Boston: Allyn and Bacon.

Heath, S. (1983). *Ways with words: Language, life, and work in communities and classrooms.* Cambridge: Cambridge University Press.

Heidegger, M. (1964). *Being and Time.* New York: Harper and Row.

Hendricks, G. and J. Fadiman, eds. (1976). *Transpersonal education: A curriculum for feeling and being.* Englewood Cliffs, NJ: Prentice-Hall, Inc.

Hessing, T. M. (2006). *Second graders' solution strategies and understanding of a combination mathematical problem.* Provo, UT: Brigham Young University.

Hewitt, J. (1984). *Self and society: A symbolic interactionist social psychology.* Boston: Allyn and Bacon.

Hewson, M. (1988). The ecological context of knowledge: implications for learning science in developing countries. *Journal of Curriculum Studies,* 20(4), pp. 317–26.

Huebner, D. (1999). *The lure of the transcendent: Collected essays by Dwayne E. Huebner.* London: Lawrence Erlbaum Associates.

Jung, C. G. (1960). *The structure and dynamics of the psyche* (R. F. C. Hull, Trans.). Princeton, NJ: Princeton University Press.

Kane, J. (Ed). (1999). *Education, information, and transformation.* Columbus, OH: Merrill/ Prentice Hall.

Kant, I. (1997). *The critique of pure reason.* Chicago: Hackett Publishing Co.

Kaulback, B. (1989). Styles of learning among Native children: A review of the research. In B. Shade (Ed.). *Culture, style, and the educative process* (pp. 137–49). Springfield, IL: Charles C. Thomas.

Kegan, R. (2000). What "form" transforms? A constructive-developmental approach to transformative learning. In J. M. Associates (Ed.), *Learning as transformation* (pp. 35-70). San Francisco: Jossey-Bass.

Kierkegaard, S. (1969). *A Kierkegaard Anthology.* R. Bretall (Ed). Princeton, NJ: Princeton University Press.

Kohut, H. (1978). *The search for self: Selected writings of Heinz Kohut: 1950–1978.* P. Ornstein (Ed.). Madison, CT: International Universities Press.

Kohlberg, L. (1987). *Child psychology and childhood education: A cognitive-developmental view.* New York: Longman.

Krashen, S. D. (1981). The "fundamental pedagogical principle" in second language teaching. *Studia Linguistica, 35*(1–2), 50–70.

Krashen, S. (1982). *Principles and practice in second language acquisition.* New York: Pergamon Press.

Krashen, S. (2003). *Explorations in language acquisition and use: The Taipei lectures.* Portsmouth, NH: Heinemann.

Kuhn, T. (1970). *The structure of scientific revolutions.* Chicago: University of Chicago Press.

Lipman, M. (1988). *Philosophy goes to school.* Philadelphia: Temple University Press.

Locke, J. (1952). *The second treatise of government.* New York: Prentice Hall.

Macdonald, J. (1995). *Theory as a prayerful act: The collected essays of James P. Macdonald.* B. Macdonald (Ed). New York: Peter Lang.

Marx, K. (1852/2010). The Eighteenth Brumaire of Louis Bonaparte. Accessed February 27, 2010: http://www.marxists.org/archive/marx/works/1852/18th-brumaire/ch01.htm .

Maslow, A. (1968). *Toward a psychology of being* (2nd edition). Princeton, NJ: D. Van Nostrand.

May, R., and Yalom, I. (1995). Existential psychotherapy. In R. Corsini & D. Wedding, (Eds.). *Current psychotherapies* (pp. 262-292). Itasca, IL: F.E. Peacock.

Mayes, C. (2004) *Seven curricular landscapes: An approach to the holistic curriculum.* Lanham, MD: University Press of America.

Mayes, C. (2007). *Understanding the whole student: Holistic multicultural education.* Lanham, MD: Rowman & Littlefield Press.

Miller, J. (1988). *The holistic curriculum.* Toronto, Ontario: Ontario Institute for Studies in Education.

More, A. (1986). Native Indian students and their learning styles: Research results and classroom applications. In B. Shade (Ed.). *Culture, style, and the educative process* (pp. 150–66). Springfield, IL: Charles C. Thomas.

Nieto, S. (2002). *Language, culture, and teaching: Critical perspectives for a new century.* Mahwah, NJ: Lawrence Erlbaum Associates.

Noddings, N. (1995). Care and moral education. In W. Kohli (Ed.), *Critical conversations in the philosophy of education* (pp. 137–48). New York: Longman.

Ornstein, A., and Hunkins, F. (1988). *Curriculum: Foundations, principles, and issues.* Boston: Allyn and Bacon.

Pepper, F. (1989). Social and cultural effects on Indian Learning style. In B. Shade (Ed.). *Culture, style, and the educative process* (pp. 137–49). Springfield, IL: Charles C. Thomas.

Piaget, J. (1966). *The moral judgment of the child.* New York: Free Press.

Pintrich, P., Marx, R., and Boyle, R. (1993). Beyond cold conceptual change: The role of motivational beliefs and classroom contextual factors in the process of conceptual change. *Review of Educational Research, 63,* 167–99.

Plato. (1991). *The Republic.* (Tr. L. Jowett). New York: Vintage.

Polacco, P. (1998a). *The keeping quilt.* New York: Simon and Schuster.

Polacco, P. (1998b). *My rotten redheaded older brother.* New York: Simon and Schuster.

Polacco, P. (1998c). *Thank you Mr. Falker.* New York: Philomel Books.

Posner, G.J., Strike, K.A., Hewson, P.W. and Gertzog, W.A. (1982). Accomodation of a scientific conception: Toward a theory of conceptual change. *Science Education,* 67(4), pp. 498–508.

Rogoff, (2003). *The cultural nature of human development.* New York: Oxford University Press.

Salzberger-Wittenberg, I. (1983).*The Emotional Experience of Learning and Teaching.* London: Routledge and Kegan Paul.

Sardello, R. and Sanders, C. (1999). Care of the senses: A neglected dimension of education. In J. Kane (Ed.). *Education, information and transformation: Essays on learning and thinking.* (pp. 226–37). Columbus, OH: Merrill/Prentice Hall.

Sartre, J. (1956). *Being and Nothingness: An Essay on Phenomenological Ontology.* New York: Philosophical Library.

Schutz, W. (1976). Education and the body. In G. Hendricks and J. Fadiman (Eds.). *Transpersonal education: A curriculum for feeling and being.* (pp. 104–10). Englewood Cliffs, New Jersey: Prentice-Hall.

Sciezka, J. (1989). *The true story of the three little pigs.* New York: Viking.

Shade, B. (1989). (Ed.) *Culture, style, and the educative process.* Springfield, IL: Charles C. Thomas.

Shalem, Y., and Bensusan, D. (1999). Why can't we stop believing? In S. Appel (Ed.), *Psychoanalysis and pedagogy* (pp. 27–44). London: Bergin and Garvey.

Solso, R. (1998). *Cognitive psychology.* Boston: Allyn and Bacon.

Spindler, G., and Spindler, L. (1987). (Eds.). *Interpretive ethnography of education: At home and abroad.* New York: Holt, Rinehart, and Winston.

Spring, J. (1976). *The sorting machine: National educational policy since 1945.* New York: David McKay Co., Inc.

Spring, J. (2003). *Deculturalization and the struggle for equality: A brief history of the education of dominated cultures in the United States.* New York: McGraw Hill.

Spronk, B. (2004). Addressing cultural diversity through learner support. In Brindley, J., Walti, C., and Zawacki-Richter, O. (Eds.), *Learner support in open, distance and online learning environments* (pp. 169–78). Oldenburg, Germany: Bibliothecksund Informationssystem der Universität Oldenburg, 2004.